An Introduction to the Israeli-Palestinian Conflict

As one of the most enduring and bitter struggles we have seen in over 100 years, the Israeli-Palestinian conflict is a powder keg, always on the verge of exploding and drawing in the wider region, the international community at large, and, in particular, the U.S. Although the conflict is of far-reaching importance, among college students and the general public there is a dearth of knowledge about it. Many of the conversations in these audiences are animated by ongoing myths and problematic talking points. This book fills in the gaps of understanding while puncturing false dichotomies and tearing down walls of ideology or indifference. It addresses perennial questions including: When and why did the conflict start? What exactly are the claims of the contending sides? Why does peace seem unattainable? What is a likely long-term outcome and how can it be brought about in a peaceful way, doing justice to both sides? Finally, this book maintains that historic Palestine, the land between the Mediterranean and the Jordan River, must become a home for both Palestinians and Jews, with equal standings for both and without exclusive claims for either. For students, scholars, and citizens of the world, this book provides a concise and level-headed way to understand one of the most complex and vexing conflicts of our time.

Akan Malici is Professor of Politics and International Affairs at Furman University. He has authored, co-authored, and co-edited numerous books, articles, and chapters on international politics and conflict, as well as on research methodology. Among the books are *U.S. Presidents and Foreign Policy Mistakes* and *Role Theory and Role Conflict in U.S.-Iran Relations*.

Praise for *An Introduction to the Israeli-Palestinian Conflict*

"This book is a crucial contribution, outlining the main issues and debates surrounding the conflict in Israel/Palestine. Especially at a time where disinformation and misconceptions abound, students and general readers interested in an academically grounded and fair assessment of the ongoing conflict would do well to read this closely."

Dana El Kurd, *University of Richmond*

An Introduction to the Israeli-Palestinian Conflict

Akan Malici

NEW YORK AND LONDON

Designed cover image: Getty/ Marcus Yam

First published 2025
by Routledge
605 Third Avenue, New York, NY 10158

and by Routledge
4 Park Square, Milton Park, Abingdon, Oxon OX14 4RN

Routledge is an imprint of the Taylor & Francis Group, an informa business

ISBN: 978-1-032-88098-3 (hbk)
ISBN: 978-0-367-25762-0 (pbk)
ISBN: 978-1-003-53626-0 (ebk)

DOI: 10.4324/9781003536260

Typeset in Sabon
by Taylor & Francis Books

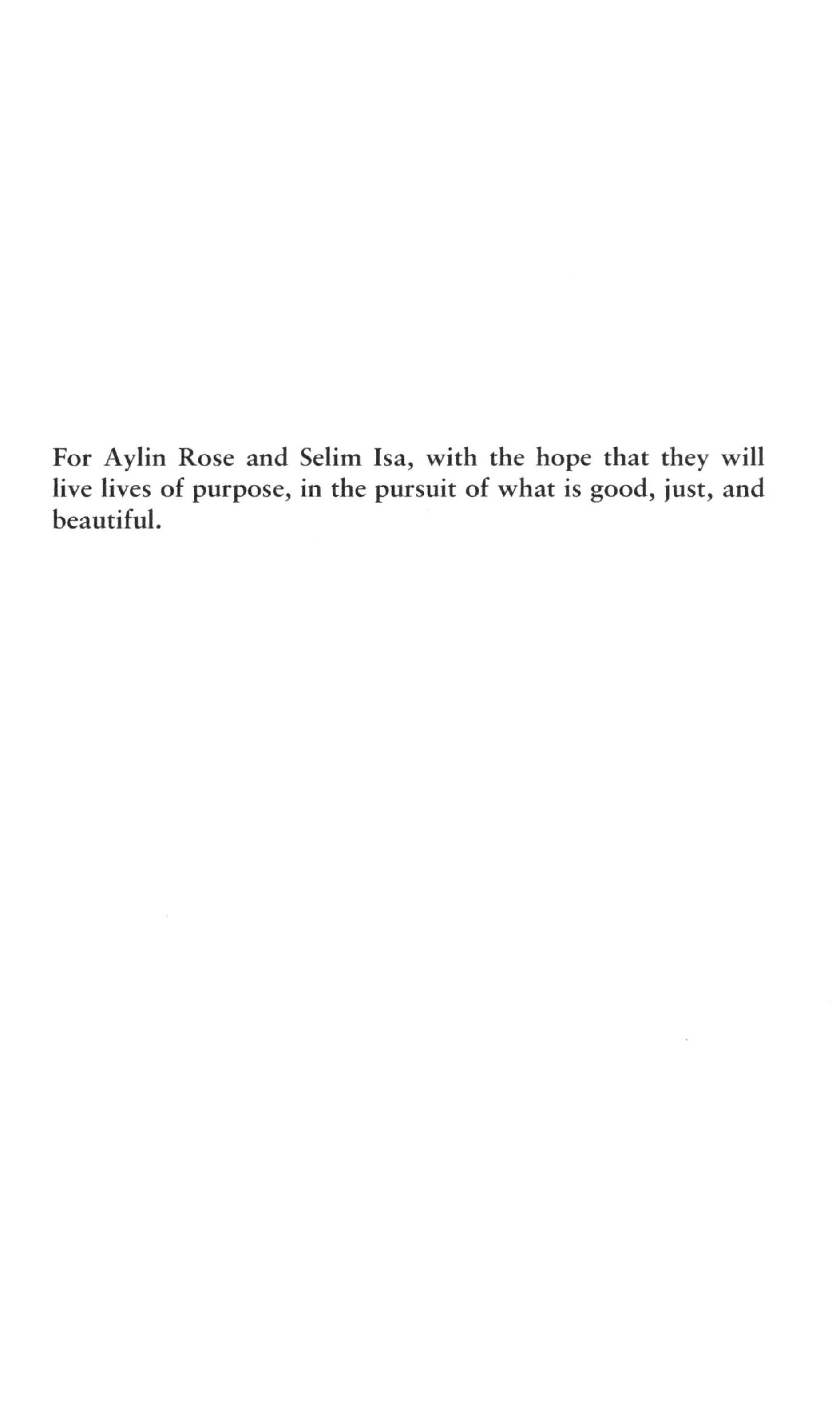

For Aylin Rose and Selim Isa, with the hope that they will live lives of purpose, in the pursuit of what is good, just, and beautiful.

Contents

Illustrations

Figure

Maps

Foreword

The successful resolution of longstanding conflicts that satisfy all parties to the conflict are rare. Grievances accumulate over time. Conflicts simmer and the pathways to a durable peace become excruciatingly difficult. Such is the case with the Israeli-Palestinian conflict. Accumulation of suspicions of the other side's intent, security concerns, and access to iconic religious sites are part of the bundle of perpetually unresolved matters as is religious nationalism. Over time, the conflict has shifted from being an Israeli-Arab conflict to being a largely Israeli-Palestinian conflict with an external patron on each side – the United States on behalf of Israel and Iran on behalf of the Palestinians. A resolution satisfactory to each side and capable of being enforced, however, remains very far from coming to fruition.

Akan Malici's thoughtful and crisply written book takes us back to the roots of this conflict even prior to the creation of the Israeli state. Two basic arguments are central to Professor Malici's thesis. The first is that the core source of conflict is about land and its proprietorship. The second is based on the Thucydides dictum that the strong dictate to the weak. The argument here is that the Israelis have always been the superior force even during its war of independence.

Both Jews and Palestinians claim proprietorship over the land. The ancient Hebraic tribes inhabited the disputed land for some time before and during the Roman Empire but were eventually scattered into a diaspora in Europe and elsewhere in the Middle East and North Africa. But the land remained sacred to Jews. Palestinians inhabited it notably during the Ottoman rule and the subsequent British mandate after World War 1. To marshal support during the war, the British government made promises to both sides that were essentially impossible to keep and ultimately too costly for a country later exhausted by the Second World War.

Zionism came on the scene in the latter part of the 19th century, largely promulgated by secular European Jews who, as a frequently persecuted minority, dreamed of a homeland where the ancient Hebrews lived and where the monuments of that ancient civilization existed. With the rise of Nazism in Germany, European Jews beat a path to Palestine in sizeable numbers. After the decimation of a great portion of European Jewry in the Holocaust, the migration to Palestine heated up and created demand for a Jewish state. That, however, came at the cost of Palestinian displacement. The continuous expansion of Israeli settlement and appropriation of land came about from the Six Day War of 1967. Though this occupation lacks international recognition, it has become *de facto* under Israeli rule, creating powerful obstacles to the emergence of a two-state solution.

Although the land is infused with other concerns such as security, religion, and so on, at its core, Malici persuasively argues, is territorial dominance, a matter that pervades much international and internal conflict.

Bert A. Rockman
Professor Emeritus of Political Science
Purdue University

Preface

The Israeli-Palestinian conflict, or the question of Palestine, as it is often referred to, is one of the most enduring and bitter struggles we have seen in over 100 years. There seems to be no end in sight in the near or intermediate future. The situation is always on the verge of renewed escalation, often drawing in the wider region, the international community, and, in particular, the United States.

Among my students as well as in public lectures, I find that there is much interest in the subject, but also very little knowledge about it. With this observation, this book seeks to fill the need for a resource available to the general reader and to undergraduate students. It is my conviction that political scientists must do better in engaging the public at large, enabling a well-informed and critical citizenry.

The questions addressed in this book are those that the common citizen brings to the topic, primarily: When and why did the conflict start? What exactly are the claims of the contending sides? Why does peace seem unattainable? What is a likely long-term outcome? Further questions address why the conflict has been so important for regional stability and what role the international community and the U.S. in particular play.

My chief ambition in this short book is to provide a good understanding of the Israeli-Palestinian conflict without the distortions that can result from simplification and brevity. My goal is for the reader to come away from the text feeling accomplished in having learned about an important issue in international politics, but also somewhat challenged and motivated to engage in reflection, or perhaps even provoked to learn more.

I am indebted to my students and public audiences who, with their ongoing interest and their many questions, have compelled me to write this book. I am deeply grateful to Dana El Kurd and Sami Hermez for their diligent reading of my manuscript and their very helpful suggestions. Special thanks go to my research assistant Sim Colson at Furman University who helped me with everything from discussing substantive points to commenting on the manuscript and editing it. Of course, I alone remain responsible for the views expressed in this book and for any errors that remain. I am very thankful to Bert Rockman for supporting my conviction in the public responsibility of scholars.

It is my pleasure to acknowledge the excellent collaboration of my Routledge editors Jennifer Kerr, Leanne Hinves, and Amelia Bashford. They showed much enthusiasm for the project as well as much patience. Jacqueline Dorsey, the editorial assistant, shepherded me very excellently through the finalization of my work. Katharine Atherton oversaw a very smooth production process and Katie Finnegan showed tremendous care in editing my manuscript. I want to thank all of them.

Most importantly, I want to thank my wife Johnna Malici for her continuous support, encouragement, and love.

Akan Malici
Greenville, South Carolina

1 Understanding the Conflict and Its Background

Our engagement with the Israeli-Palestinian conflict begins in a seemingly unlikely place and time, in ancient Greece. Here we encounter the famous historian Thucydides, and engaging briefly with him will allow us to learn some fundamental lessons about international politics and conflict. His work remains admired and authoritative for insights into perpetual issues of international politics and conflict. This is also the case for the Israeli-Palestinian conflict as we will see throughout this book.

Thucydides was born around 460 BCE in Athens. He grew up as a member of the elite, witnessing the great period in Greek history when democracy was established in Athens. Also at this time, the foundations for Western philosophy and science were laid and politics, like many other areas of existence, became subject to rational inquiry.[1] As fate would have it, scrutinizing politics became Thucydides' vocation. In 431 BCE, the Peloponnesian War began and would last until 404 BCE. When it broke out, he was certain it would be a war of great importance, worthy of being chronicled in detail.

Thus, he began recording it immediately, his writings ultimately becoming the famous *History of the Peloponnesian War*. It remained Thucydides' only book, but it was an outstanding work as he engaged in a systematic method of evidence collection and analysis. Although he couldn't have anticipated that centuries later he would be regarded as the first scientific historian, he was nevertheless convinced that his work would remain relevant for all times. Indeed, around the world, students of international conflict continue to begin their classes by reading Thucydides' text. What are some of the important insights he has to teach us?

We will begin this chapter by answering this question. From there we will venture into a brief overview of some basics about the conflicting sides, Israelis and Palestinians. Subsequently, we will see that the conflict is primarily over land and not over religion. Having said this, the land that we are talking about *is* the Holy Land and, of course, it does have

DOI: 10.4324/9781003536260-1

religious significance, and we shall consider that too. It won't surprise anyone that Jews, on the one hand, and Palestinians, on the other, have different stories to tell about the conflict and their claims to the Holy Land. This aspect also deserves to be laid out in this introductory chapter. I will close this chapter by charting the path through the book.

Ancient Insights for a Contemporary Conflict

One of the most discussed episodes in the *History of the Peloponnesian War* is the Melian Dialogue, which occurred in 416 BCE. The powerful city-state of Athens intended to conquer the weaker island of Melos and own it as one of its colonies. The inhabitants of Melos, however, hoped to preserve their independence. At a meeting between the leaders of Athens and Melos a verbal contest ensued. After some initial back and forth, the Athenians were not persuaded by the Melians' arguments and stated,

> [W]e recommend that you should try to get what is possible for you to get, taking into consideration what we both really do think; since you know as well as we do that, when the matters are discussed by practical people, the standard of justice depends on the equality of power to compel and that in fact *the strong do what they have the power to do and the weak accept what they have to accept.* [2]

The Athenians attempted to convince the Melians to submit now rather than face Athenian power soon after. Whether or not the Melians actually submitted, so the Athenians reasoned, their power would ensure that Melos was awaiting the same outcome, namely Athenian domination. The Melians resisted and drew upon arguments of morality and justice, arguing,

> Then in our view (since you force us to leave justice out of account and to confine ourselves to self-interest) – in our view it is at any rate useful that you should not destroy a principle that is to the general good of all men – namely, that in the case of all who fall into danger *there should be such a thing as fair play and just dealing* ...

After Athenian representatives repeatedly urged their Melian counterparts to give in, they withdrew from the discussion and the Melians were left to themselves in their final consultations. Concluding these, they responded to the Athenians, "Our decision, Athenians, is just the same as it was at first. We are not prepared to give up in a short moment the liberty which our city has enjoyed from its foundation for 700 years."

The Melians had hope and confidence that they could prevail in the coming war. But they could not.

It was as the Athenians said: The strong did what they had the power to do, and the weak, ultimately, accepted what they had to accept. Since Thucydides' famous recording of this dialogue, international relations scholars have claimed that the essence of this exchange has remained true throughout history and that it will also remain true in the future: Power is the paramount force in international politics and it trumps considerations of law, justice, and fairness.

This edict also applies to the Israeli-Palestinian conflict. Before this conflict came into full being in 1948, it was major European powers that set the background for it. After the Second World War, the Cold War's two superpowers had considerable bearing on the conflict, with the U.S., however, being far more involved than the Soviet Union. Thus, throughout this book, it will be important for us to keep an eye on how powerful states have impacted and continue to impact the conflict between Israelis and Palestinians. We will also pay attention to the involvement of regional states.

Our main focus, of course, will be on the main protagonists in the conflict: Israelis and Palestinians. In this relationship, Israel has been the manifestly more powerful side and it has thus been able to determine the outcome at many critical junctures. It is, however, not the case that the more powerful side committed all the injustices in the conflict. As we will see, both sides committed atrocities throughout the duration of the conflict and into the present. With this we will also see that while the powerful do as they have the power to do, the weak do not necessarily just accept their predicament. In the Peloponnesian War, the Melians did resist as they could. Palestinians have also resisted, within the realm of their possibilities. But while Palestinians have maintained a strong sense of their national identity and received increasing international recognition, a Palestinian state has remained absent.

How to judge who is more powerful, at least historically and in conventional ways, is relatively straightforward. It is usually the side with the bigger military, more artillery, more aircraft, and so on. How to judge what is just and unjust can be more difficult. What may appear unjust to one person may be just to another person and, among other things, it has to do with the experiences and convictions one is bringing to the question. Hence, although I will make statements about matters of justice at the end of each chapter, the reader must not take them as authoritative verdicts. Instead, they should be prompted to further reflect and engage with the issues presented here, especially because there are diverging accounts and contending perspectives. Now, let's delve deeper into the Israeli-Palestinian conflict, starting with the basics.

Some Basics About the Enemies

It is important to know that long before there was the Israeli-Palestinian conflict, there was no State of Israel, nor were there Palestinians seeking their own state. When the conflict first began germinating in the late 19th century, the land in question was part of a province of the Ottoman Empire and it was referred to as Palestine. This is when our account of the conflict will begin, although we will briefly go back into a far more distant history to illustrate the Jewish and Palestinian religious connections to the land. After the end of the First World War, Great Britain assumed control over the contested land. It now came to be geographically clearly demarcated and referred to as the British Mandate of Palestine.

The area that Israelis and Palestinians have been quarrelling and fighting over is small. It extends from Lebanon in the north to the Gulf of Aqaba and the Sinai Peninsula in the south and from the Mediterranean Sea in the west to the Jordan River in the east, where it borders the countries of Syria and Jordan. The area is just over 10,000 square miles large and equals roughly the size of Maryland, one of the United States' smallest states. The British Mandate lasted until 1948, when the State of Israel came into being. At first, it comprised about 55 percent of what was the Mandate, but it expanded over time and now comprises about 80 percent. The remaining 20 percent or so are often referred to as the Palestinian Territories, comprised of the West Bank and Gaza. The West Bank is referred to as such because it is on the west bank of the Jordan River and the Dead Sea.

In this book, when talking about the contested land before 1948, I will refer to it as the Mandate of Palestine, Historic Palestine, or simply Palestine. From 1948 onwards, I will distinguish between Israel and the Palestinian Territories. Map 1.1 illustrates what we have covered so far.

There are just over 9 million people living in Israel and about 2 million of them are Arabs (mostly Palestinian). In the West Bank (including East Jerusalem), there are about 3.3 million Palestinians and about 700,000 Jewish settlers. Many Palestinians live in or near the main cities of the West Bank, namely Nablus, Ramallah, Hebron, and Jericho. Jews in the West Bank live in settlements which, according to international law, are illegal. In Gaza there are about 2.2 million Palestinians, living in a tiny sliver of land that is about 25 miles long and 5 miles wide. It constitutes one of the most densely populated territories in the world. More than two thirds of its inhabitants are refugees. So, in total, the land known as Mandatory Palestine after the First World War comprises today about 15 million inhabitants, with an about equal share of Jews

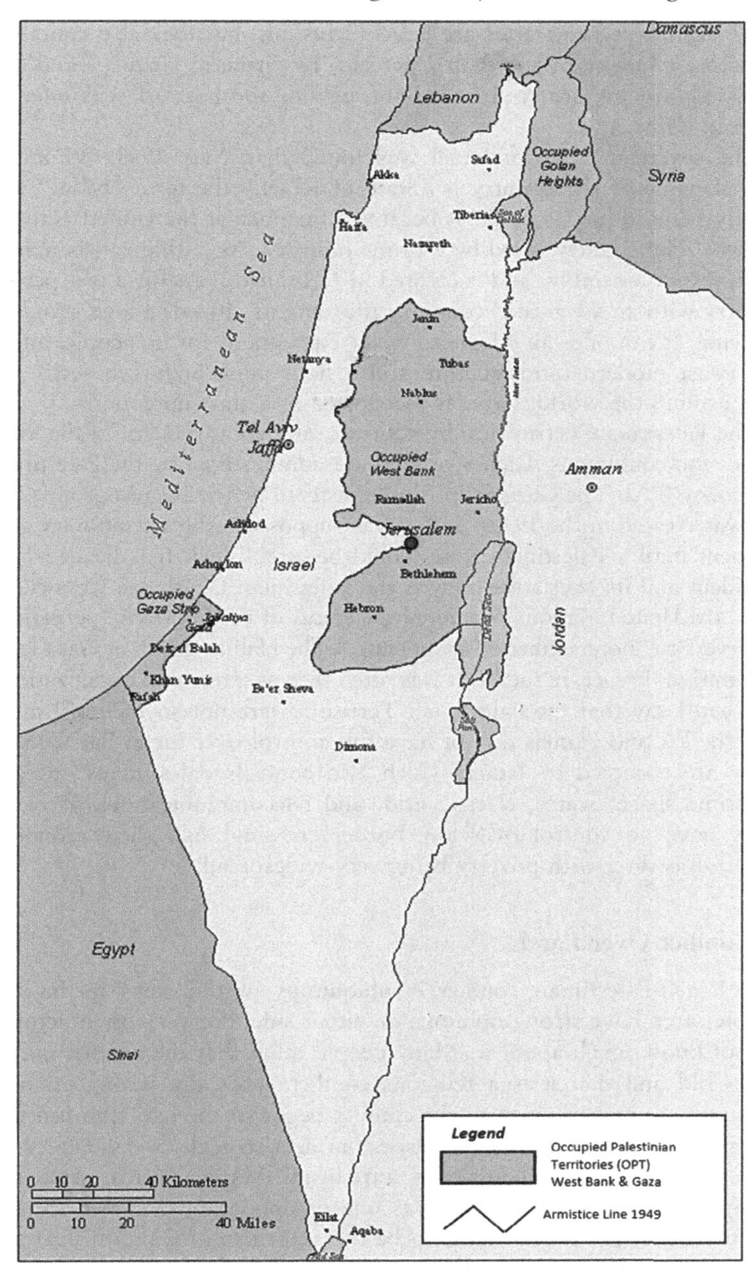

Map 1.1 Israel and the Occupied Territories
Source: Adapted from a map from the Israeli Committee Against House Demolition, used with permission. The original map can be found at https://icahd.org/map2/

and Palestinians. The latter are largely Muslims, but they also contain a Christian minority of less than 2 percent. By virtue of language and culture, Palestinians are Arabs, and throughout the book, I will refer to them in both ways.

The sovereign State of Israel was founded in May 1948. While the formal name of the country is "State of Israel," the term "Israel" will mostly be used in this book. It became a member of the United Nations in 1949. The country is led by a prime minister. Its parliament is named the *Knesset* (assembly) and is located in Jerusalem. Israel is a prosperous country with an advanced economy, affording its citizens a high standard of living. It can offer an advanced welfare programs for its people, and it can boast modern infrastructure and a flourishing high-tech sector. In fact, around the world, Israel is recognized as a start-up country.

The Palestinian Territories, by contrast, are not sovereign. In the West Bank, non-contiguous patches of land are administered by the Palestinian Authority (PA). The Gaza Strip is administered by the Hamas group. The PA was created in the 1990s, and it was supposed to be a temporary government until a Palestinian state would be established. It is headed by a president and its legislative body is the Palestinian Legislative Council. In 2012, the United Nations promoted the status of the PA from "permanent observer" to "nonmember observer state." The Hamas group in Gaza lacks recognition; in fact, in the West it is often seen as a terrorist organization.

When I say that the Palestinian Territories are not sovereign, I mean that the PA and Hamas do not have full control over them. Far from it. They are occupied by Israel, which also controls Palestinians' air and maritime space, water, electric grid, and telecommunications network. They have no control over any border crossings and their economic situation is dire, with poverty being very widespread.

A Conflict Over Land

The Israeli-Palestinian conflict is ubiquitous in the news media and people often have strong opinions on either side, but very often actually do not know much about it. Many people think that the conflict is centuries old and that it is a religious conflict. They are wrong on both accounts. As just mentioned, the conflict began in the late 19th century, and it did so not over religious issues but as a struggle over land.

In fact, the conflict didn't even start in the Middle East; it started in Europe. There, Jewish history was one of oppression and persecution. For centuries, Jews were made to be the scapegoats for the misfortunes of European Christians as they were confronted with stereotypes, prejudice, exclusion, and hate. Beginning in the 16th century, some towns created ghettos to which Jews were restricted. With the onset of the dreadful pogroms in the Russian Empire and Eastern Europe in the late 19th and early 20th century, the situation got yet so much worse. "Pogrom" is a Russian word and it means "to wreak havoc." The pogroms included the looting of Jewish homes and businesses, the destruction of their property, and countless violent attacks and massacres. Ultimately, Jews would come to face the horrors of the Holocaust. Six million Jews perished.

Such dire historic circumstances in Europe compelled Jews to seek a new homeland. This desire emanated in the late 19th century, beginning with a few Jews who came to be known as Zionists. We will explore this term in more detail in the next chapter. Here it shall suffice to know that these Zionists laid claim to Palestine. At that time, the Palestinian population was predominantly Muslim, with about 10 percent being Christian and about 5 percent being Jewish. Many Zionists considered Judaism not to be confined to a religion; it was equal to nationhood. In fact, their primary motivation for a homeland in Palestine was not religious but nationalistic. On the eve of the First World War, the ambition for a Jewish homeland in Palestine found the support of British imperialists for reasons we will also consider in the next chapter. As waves of Jewish mass immigration followed, this led to tensions and ultimately also conflicts with the native Palestinians.

This, in short, is how the Israeli-Palestinian conflict started in the late 19th century, and not many centuries ago as is often assumed. That it began as a territorial conflict and remained that for a long time was also expressed straightforwardly by Israel's famous first prime minister David Ben-Gurion. Some years before he became Israel's leader, he explained in rather simple terms, "We and they [the Arabs] want the same thing: We both want Palestine. And that is the fundamental conflict."[3] For the many centuries before there was Jewish mass immigration to Palestine, the Muslim majority and the Christian and Jewish minorities lived in peace with each other. No one saw a religious ordinance to be in a religious conflict with the other.

Once the conflict began manifesting itself more strongly, however, around the 1920s, it did take on religious dimensions, at first sparingly and then increasingly more. For example, since the 1967 War, a growing number of Jews have been referring to the Palestinian West Bank with the biblical designation Judea and Samaria and are thus laying a religious claim to the land. Equally, the rise of the Palestinian Hamas in the 1980s brought with it religiously underlined claims to the land. Moreover, in the history of the conflict, the holy sites in Jerusalem have also been focal points and ever more do the inflammatory words and deeds of both sides draw much international attention.

While recognizing these religious dimensions, it is very important to state strongly that they are not innate to the conflict. There is nothing in the conflicting parties' sacred scriptures that would dictate a ceaseless conflict toward each other. Framing the conflict as a religious one is not only incorrect, but also dangerous as it contributes to a worldview where the world's great religions are in a clash with each other. They are not.

The Religious Significance of the Land

Having said that the conflict is, at root, a modern territorial conflict, it is also the case that the land is very significant to Jews, Christians, and Muslims alike. Before it became holy to any of them, the land was known as Canaan and it included the area west and east of the Jordan River. That this land would become sacred to Jews, Christians, and Muslims is of little surprise, in good part because all three of these religions are Abrahamic faiths and share a belief in various of God's messengers who succeeded the Prophet Abraham and have lived and preached in this land. Since Judaism predates both Christianity and Islam, it makes sense to begin discussing the significance of the land for Jews. It is important to point out that what we will encounter in the next paragraphs is not a historical analysis; instead, we're considering the three-faith tradition's ideational connection to the land by reference to holy texts and figures.

To illustrate their ancient connection to the land, Jews often refer to verses 12:1 and 12:7 in the Book of Genesis, the first book of the Hebrew Bible. God says to Abraham, "Go from your native land ... to the place I will show you." Abraham obeys and God explains further, "I will assign this land to your offspring." For Jews, these revelations often represent the scriptural moment that gives birth to the Jewish people. The place that God shows to Abraham is Canaan and it becomes the "Promised Land" for Jews. They come to see themselves as God's chosen people and in Canaan they were to build a commonwealth based on God's law. Yet, before it could come to the realization of this divine mandate, a devastating famine forced them into exile in Egypt where they would suffer from the oppression of the terrible Pharaoh.[4]

In Egypt, the descendants of Abraham grew into a people with various tribes – the Israelites. Moses freed them from the Pharaoh and although he died before his people would enter the Promised Land, he led them to its borders. Under the leadership of Joshua, the Israelites engaged in a military campaign, conquered the land, and settled there. The establishment of the Israelite monarchy came in the latter half of the 11th century and the greatest glory was experienced with the kingships of David and his son Solomon in the 10th century BCE. King David is remembered for conquering further lands, including Jerusalem, and King Solomon is revered as a wise leader and, of course, for the building of the First Temple (also known as Solomon's Temple), where he is also believed to have placed the Ark of the Covenant. The temple became the center of Jewish religious life.

After Solomon's death, the kingdom became divided into the Kingdom of Israel (in the north) and the Kingdom Judah (in the south). Beginning in the late eighth century both kingdoms were starting to lose their independence to powerful neighbors. In 587 BCE, the Babylonian King Nebuchadnezzar invaded Jerusalem and destroyed Solomon's Temple. Jews were exiled but were ultimately restored to Palestine by the Persians in 539 BCE. The Temple was rebuilt, albeit on a much smaller scale. It was only under King Herod, in 19 BCE, that the building was expanded to greater scale and magnificence. Then the Romans came to occupy the land, however, and General Titus destroyed the Temple in 70 CE, hoping to put an end to Judaism's challenge to the Pagan Roman Empire. The destruction brought the end to any hope of a second Jewish Commonwealth. What today is known as the Western Wall (or the Wailing Wall) is a remnant of the Second Temple.

Jews were banished from Jerusalem, and it was only with the Muslim conquest of Jerusalem in 638 CE that they were permitted back into the city. The small Jewish minority that came to live in Palestine was encouraged by Arab rule because Muslims accepted the revelations of both Judaism and Christianity as divine. Compared to former Roman and Byzantine governors, under Arab Muslims the Jewish population was granted significant autonomy. Yet, in the centuries that followed the vast majority of Jews never came to live in Palestine again. Instead, they lived "turning to the land." Illustrating their ideational connection, synagogues across the world were oriented toward Jerusalem and for many centuries now Jews have been singing "next year in Jerusalem" at the end of Passover Seder.[5]

Jerusalem and the lands surrounding it also figures very importantly in the Christian faith tradition, of course. Most important for Christians is that Jesus was born in Bethlehem, just south of Jerusalem, and it remains an important destination for Christian pilgrims. As an infant, Christians believe, Jesus was occasionally brought to Jerusalem and, according to the Gospel of Luke, he was "presented" at the Temple. This occasion marks the ceremonial circumcision of the first-born son on their eighth day. Upon assuming his ministry, Jesus came to preach in Jerusalem, particularly at the Temple courts. This is also the place where Jesus warned against corruption, and at Passover he overturned the tables and expelled the merchants and moneychangers who had turned the place into a den of thieves.

Jerusalem has further significance for Christians because it is the site of the Passion, Jesus' final suffering, his crucifixion and his resurrection. He was made to carry the cross on the Via Delarosa onto the Hill of Cavalry where he was then nailed to it, according to Christian faith. About 300 years after Jesus' crucifixion, the Church of the Holy Sepulcher was dedicated on this site and it contains Jesus' empty tomb. The church is located in Jerusalem's Christian quarter and, like Bethlehem, it is a major destination for pilgrims to witness and to pray for redemption.

Finally, Jerusalem and the land beyond is also very significant in the Islamic tradition. In fact, part of its significance derives from previous prophets' association with Jerusalem – Abraham, David, Solomon, and Jesus among them. The prophet of Islam is Muhammad, and Muslims believe that God summoned him to Jerusalem. The Qur'an, Islam's sacred scripture, states, "Glory to Him who journeyed His servant by night, from the sacred place of prayer, to the farthest place of prayer, whose precincts We have blessed, in order to show him of Our wonders." The servant in the verse is Muhammad. The sacred place of prayer is the *Masjid al-Haram* in Mecca (in today's Saudi Arabia) and when the Qur'an speaks of the farthest place of prayer (*Al Masjid al-Aqsa*), Muslims understand this to be in Jerusalem.

Upon reaching Jerusalem in a miraculous night journey, Muhammad is leading other prophets in prayer and is then invited by God to an ascent into the heavens. As he is reaching the highest point, he is blessed with the experience of the Divine Presence and he obtains directives for Islamic supplications. Today, the site of Muhammad's ascent is contained in the most notable buildings in Jerusalem, namely the Dome of the Rock and just a few steps away is the Masjid al-Qibli. Both buildings are part of a compound known to Muslims as *Masjid al-Aqsa* or the *Haram al-Sharif* (the Noble Sanctuary). Because of the Haram's outstanding religious significance, it continues to be a major pilgrimage site for Muslims from all over the world.

In concluding this section, it is important to note that Jews refer to the *Haram al-Sharif* as Temple Mount and believe the site to have been the locale of their ancient temples. Since 1967 and especially in more recent years, these contending religious claims have contributed to serious escalations between Jews and Palestinians.

Contending Narratives

Anyone who has ever attended a panel event on the Israeli-Palestinian conflict with speakers representing both sides will know that there are contending, yes, clashing narratives about the conflict. The panelists are likely to disagree at many junctures of the conversation. They may well disagree on why something happened and how it happened, and sometimes they may go as far as to disagree on what happened. There is, in other words, an Israeli narrative with its typical highlights, interpretations, and omissions and there is the equivalent on the Palestinian side.

The Israeli narrative often begins by emphasizing that Jews have maintained close religious ties to the land for at least 3,000 years. This place gave rise not only to their religion, but also to their nationhood. Hence, Jews say, they have a religious and a historical claim. In modern times, the Israeli narrative is perhaps best encapsulated by the famous Hebrew phrase *miShoah leTekuma* – 'from Holocaust to rebirth.'[6] The narrative emphasizes centuries of antisemitism and Jewish suffering in Europe. It got yet worse in the late 19th century as it came to the violent pogroms mentioned above. They were a disaster, but as it tragically turned out, they were only forerunners to the ultimate catastrophe of the Holocaust.

As the Jewish predicament was worsening in the latter part of the 19th century, it led to the emergence of Zionist thought – the idea that the Jewish people constitute a nation and need a homeland that is solely theirs. It was a nationalist liberation movement away from the dangers of life in Europe. Thus, Palestine was to become the land of refuge for tens of thousands of European Jews. It was not just any refuge, however; it was the biblically promised land that should now be redeemed. Palestine was seen as largely uninhabited, as exemplified by the statement that is often cited in the literature, namely that Palestine was "a land without people for a people without a land."

As more and more Jews fled Europe and settled in Palestine, tensions with Palestinians emerged. The narrative points to Jewish readiness to compromise and to make peace while pointing to the other side's repeated failures to do so. This began in the 1920s, when Palestinians rejected proposals for joint Jewish-Palestinian governing bodies. It continued with a 1937 British partition plan according to which Palestinians would have received most of the land. A decade later, in 1947, Palestinians also rejected the United Nations partition plan. The Israeli narrative highlights further that since the country's founding in 1948, it has been surrounded by hostile countries and had to defend its right to exist in several wars over the decades.

Palestinians, in contrast, emphasize that, in fact, they are the contested land's indigenous people, originating from the Canaanites and the Philistines.[7] With the advent of Islam since the seventh century, most Palestinians, over time, became Muslims. Like Jews, they also emphasize religious bonds to the land that emerged with the ascent of Islam in the seventh century. Moreover, Palestinians point out that it was them who had reestablished Jews in Jerusalem after they were expelled by the Romans in the first century CE, and also that for many centuries they have lived peacefully alongside Jewish minorities. Thus, so Palestinians say, they have no issues at all with Jews and Judaism. Instead, their quarrel is with Zionism. From early on, this European ideology was seen as an existential threat. They also counter the Zionist narrative about the land being empty. In fact, it had almost 1,000 villages, a progressive urban elite, and much historical and cultural richness and vibrancy.

While Zionism may have presented itself as a national liberation movement for European Jews, for Palestinians it meant a denial of their right to national self-determination and the eviction from their beloved homeland for the benefit of foreign settlers. Acknowledging the dire predicament of Jews in Europe, Palestinians add that they bore no responsibility for it. Yet, they complain bitterly, they had to pay the price for it and continue to do so. The British are seen as particularly perfidious in this injustice as they appropriated Zionism toward their imperial machinations so as to extend British rule over Arab lands. From here on, the Palestinian narrative becomes one of resistance against the British Empire, which had betrayed its promise of Arab independence, as well as against Jewish mass immigration and progressing dispossessions.

Whether it was the 1920s proposals for joint governance, the 1937 British partition plan or the United Nations partition plan from 1947, the Palestinians see them all as imperialist impositions. These plans were equivalent to the stealing of Palestinian homeland. The 1948 Arab-Israeli War led to more than 700,000 Palestinian refugees who Israel does not permit to return to their homes. This event is often referred to as *al-Nakba* (the catastrophe) and, for Palestinians, it continues to unfold into the present. The refugee number has swollen to about six million and the Palestinian plight is marked by an ongoing occupation, land confiscations, house demolitions, expanding Israeli settlements, and a separation wall built on long stretches of Palestinian lands, robbing the people of their rights and dignity.

Of course, there is so much more to be said about each narrative and what we would find is a continued divergence on many issues. As we're maneuvering ourselves through the history of the Israeli-Palestinian conflict into the present, we will be guided by rigorous and authoritative scholarly materials that will help us establish a good understanding of it. My goal is that the reader will come away feeling accomplished to have learned about an issue that will continue to occupy a prominent place in the news for years to come. I also hope that the reader will come away somewhat challenged and motivated to engage in reflection and perhaps even provoked to learn more.

The Way Forward

In this chapter, we have learned some basics about the Israeli-Palestinian conflict. It is neither a religious conflict, nor have Jews and Palestinians been fighting for centuries. Their conflict started as a struggle over land. In other words, Jews and Palestinians are not born enemies to each other. The hostility can and has been intense, however, and through the remainder of the book we will learn in more detail how exactly the conflict started, how it deepened and what some future scenarios might look like.

In Chapter 2, I will elaborate on what I have alluded to already in this introduction, namely that the Israeli-Palestinian conflict has its roots in Europe. Jews had long been persecuted in Europe and long-standing antisemitism culminated in pogroms in the late 19th century. These experiences led to the emergence of political Zionism, which is in essence Jewish nationalism, and it manifested itself as the aspiration to establish a Jewish nation-state in Palestine.

In Chapter 3, I will discuss how the Zionist movement grew stronger in the early 20th century. Coinciding with European imperial machinations in the Middle East during the First World War, the Holy Land became the embattled land. The onset of Nazism in Germany, the Second World War, and the horrors of the Holocaust had further tremendous impact on the situation. As Jewish insistence for a state in Palestine intensified, the U.S. led the United Nations to issue a partition plan in 1947.

In Chapter 4, I will begin with the establishment of the State of Israel in 1948. Immediately afterwards, the first Arab-Israeli War began, involving several Arab countries. Israel prevailed and henceforth encompassed nearly 80 percent of what had been Palestine. Significant events that followed were the 1956 Suez War, the 1964 founding of the Palestine Liberation Organization (PLO), and the 1967 War. Through its spectacular victory in this war, Israel came to occupy 100 percent of historic Palestine.

In Chapter 5, I will begin with Israel's expansion after the 1967 War and the increase in Palestinian armed resistance. In 1973, Syria and Egypt aimed at recovering their lost territories, but largely failed. While Palestinians made some international diplomatic progress as the decade advanced, it was only Egypt and Israel that attained a U.S.-brokered peace deal. The occupation of Palestinian territories continued and in the latter half of the 1980s it led to a Palestinian uprising.

In Chapter 6, I will discuss how, in 1988, the Palestinian leadership recognized Israel's legitimate existence and called for the creation of a sovereign Palestinian state alongside Israel. In 1993, it came to the Oslo

Accords. These established a mutual recognition between the Israeli government and the PLO. Within a five-year process a final resolution was to be reached. In effect, however, nothing changed. Further diplomatic attempts followed, but also these remained fruitless.

In Chapter 7, I will review the recent past of the conflict. Through many decades the U.S. aided Israel in significant ways and, in fact, in the last years this support has only increased. Israel has been the more powerful side for decades and it was able to impose its will. However, this came at a painful price, namely the accumulation of human rights violations against Palestinians and a situation where Israel in now widely described as an apartheid regime.

In Chapter 8, I will discuss the various possible outcomes to the Israeli-Palestinian conflict, the one-state outcome and the two-state outcome, as well as some implications. I will conclude with the U.S. role in the future of the conflict.

Notes

1 Rex Warner and Abid Hussain. 1959. "Thucydides." *Indian Literature* 2: 50–53.
2 This quote and the following ones are from Thucydides. 1972. *History of the Peloponnesian War*. New York: Penguin Books, pp. 402–407 (italics added).
3 Quoted in Avi Shlaim. 2014. *The Iron Wall*. New York: W.W. Norton & Company, p. 19.
4 Daniel Gordis. 2016. *Israel: A Concise History of a Nation Reborn*. New York: HarperCollins Publishers, pp. 32–34. The following paragraphs draw heavily on Daniel Gordis, *Israel: A Concise History of a Nation Reborn*, pp. 32–44, Mark Tessler. 2009. *A History of the Israeli-Palestinian Conflict*. Bloomington, IN: Indiana University Press, pp. 7–16, and Gudrun Krämer. 2008. *A History of Palestine*. Princeton, NJ: Princeton University Press, pp. 5–15.
5 Gudrun Krämer, *A History of Palestine*, p. 25; Daniel Gordis, *Israel: A Concise History of a Nation Reborn*, p. 44.
6 Ian Black. 2017. *Enemies and Neighbors: Arabs and Jews in Palestine and Israel, 1917–2017*. New York: Atlantic Monthly Press, p. 3.
7 Mark Tessler, *A History of the Israeli-Palestinian Conflict*, p. 69.

2 A Conflict Made in Europe

Theodor Herzl was born in 1860 in the Hungarian city of Pest. He was from a well-off Jewish family and when he reached adulthood, the family moved to Vienna, Austria. His upbringing was secular, and he had an ambivalent relationship to his Jewish heritage. Living in one of Europe's cultural metropolises, he even aimed at shedding his Jewish traits so that he would be more accepted in European society. When Herzl attended law school and experienced widespread antisemitism, things would gradually change, however. Although he did graduate with a law degree, Herzl's real passion was writing. In 1891, he became the Paris reporter for the Viennese newspaper *Neue Freie Presse* and soon he would witness the Dreyfus Affair, which would seal his new calling.

The affair centered on Alfred Dreyfus, a French officer of Jewish heritage. In 1894, Dreyfus was accused of relaying military secrets to Germany and was thus charged with treason. Upon his conviction, the crowds chanted, "Down with the Jews." Herzl was among those who believed that Dreyfus had been framed. Dreyfus was indeed innocent, but he spent several years in prison nevertheless. Despite finally being exonerated in 1906, the case illustrated the alleged disloyalty Jews continued to be accused of and that antisemitism was very much alive, even in France, the land that had pledged liberty, equality, and brotherhood. This event convinced Herzl that for most Jews it was impossible to assimilate into European society. Jews had to have their own homeland, and Herzl dedicated the remainder of his life to this end.

The Imperial Powers and the Question of Palestine

Although Herzl deliberated various locations for a Jewish homeland, it ultimately had to be in Palestine. He knew that such an ambition could be accomplished only with the support of a great power. He thus traveled to Istanbul, the capital of the Ottoman Empire, which held

DOI: 10.4324/9781003536260-2

Palestine as one of its provinces. In return for a Jewish homeland there, Herzl promised very considerable amounts of Jewish capital, which would help the Sultan's increasingly bankrupt government. Herzl also approached the German Kaiser for help. A Jewish state in Palestine would be beneficial to Europe, he wrote, because it would "form a portion of a rampart of Europe against Asia, an outpost of civilization as opposed to barbarism."[1] Despite his intense efforts, at this moment, Herzl was unable to gain any meaningful support.

Yet, in due time this would change. The Ottoman Empire had been weakening for decades and this posed the so-called *Eastern Question*. The question pertained to the empire's falling territories for which imperial contest ensued among Britain, France, Spain, and Italy. Britain and France were both very powerful and they came to dominate this contest. Already in the 1830s Great Britain had laid claim on Aden in the Arabian Peninsula and France began to dominate Algeria. Later in the century, France claimed Tunisia, and Britain extended its claim on Egypt. At the beginning of the 20th century, Britain established a powerful presence in Persia (Iran) and in 1912 France claimed northern Morocco.

Britain was the world's economic super-power and arguably it had the greatest interest in the Middle East. Its main goal was to secure land and sea routes to its most valuable colonial holdings in India. The land route led through Ottoman-controlled territory and the sea route led through the Suez Canal in Egypt, connecting the Mediterranean Sea to the Pacific Ocean. Just a few decades after Britain had begun occupying Egypt, a new opportunity presented itself: should the Ottoman Empire indeed collapse further, Palestine would become a desired future acquisition. France, in the meantime, also laid its eyes ever more on the Middle East.

This is a brief look at the landscape of international power politics as the question of Palestine began to formulate itself at the end of the 19th century. While there was, at this time, no powerful European patron to support a Jewish homeland in Palestine, the British showed a general sympathy for Herzl's quest and, in 1903, offered land in its East Africa colonies instead. However, as the years progressed and as the Ottoman Empire was coming to an end, the British came to calculate that a Jewish homeland in Palestine would grant them control of Palestine.

The Jewish Predicament in Europe

For centuries, Jews had suffered harshly in Europe. It is worthwhile to quote a passage from an 1899 essay by Mark Twain published in *Harper's Magazine*:

> [T]he Jew is being legislated out of Russia ... Spain [decided] to banish him four hundred years ago, and Austria about a couple centuries later. In all the ages Christian Europe has ... curtail[ed] his activities ... Trade after trade was taken away from the Jew by statue till practically none was left. He was forbidden to engage in agriculture; he was forbidden to practice law; he was forbidden to practice medicine, except among Jews; he was forbidden the handicrafts. Even the seats of learning and the schools of science had to be closed against this tremendous antagonist.[2]

While the predicament for Jews in Europe had indeed been adverse for centuries, in the aftermath of the French Revolution, matters actually seemed to be improving somewhat. Of all the political, social, and economic barriers Jews had experienced, the most significant one was that they had not been granted equal standing before the law or citizenship in the countries they had resided in. In 1789, however, the French National Assembly granted citizenship to Jews. Gradually, Jews also achieved a new standing in other European countries. In the historical literature on the Jewish situation in Europe, this process is often described as *Jewish Emancipation*. To be sure, there were continuous setbacks, but overall the situation seemed to improve.

Alongside this legal emancipation came an intellectual and cultural emancipation, known as the *haskalah*, or the Jewish Enlightenment. At the base of it was a fundamental dissatisfaction with the Jewish present and outlook. Adherents of the *haskalah* were referred to as *maskilim*, meaning the 'enlightened ones.' They contended that Jews must move beyond their traditional and narrow emphasis on religious doctrines toward a secular and worldly-rational attitude. It is through this emancipation that Jews would reduce cultural obstacles to integration. In short, the ambition of the *haskalah* was nothing less than the forging of a new Jewry.[3]

Jewish integration in European societies did in fact progress in the 19th century. Jews were very often accomplished professionals, scholars, and scientists and also the heads of relevant intellectual and social movements. However, there were also stark reminders that the situation had not improved sufficiently. Jews had long served as scapegoats for Europe's problems. In Germany, for example, where Jews had assumed high-ranking positions in finance and trade, they were blamed for the country's economic woes in the 1870s. Already in 1862 did the prominent Jewish thinker Moses Hess have a pessimistic outlook on the apparent progress, commenting that "despite enlightenment and emancipation, the Jew in exile who denies his nationality will never earn the respect of the nations among whom he dwells."[4]

In Eastern Europe, where about 80 percent of the European Jewry resided, the situation had not improved much to begin with. Millions of Jews continued to be restricted to live a life of poverty in the Pale of Settlement, a region between the Black Sea and the Baltic. Vile antisemitism reignited in the second half of the 19th century. Pogroms had occurred before, but now they widened and intensified in their violence while government authorities simply stood by or even encouraged them. Terror on Jews unfolded in Odessa, Warsaw, Kiev, and in other places. About two and a half million Jews were forced to leave Eastern Europe by the beginning of the First World War. Many desired to go to America and many emigrated to Western European countries. Only a few went to Palestine.[5]

The Factor of Christian Zionism

In this dire context, some European Jews started thinking more about the need for their own homeland where they could be safe. Notably, many of these Jews were not very pious. Their thoughts and ideas came to be known as Zionism. To be precise though, the term should be *political* Zionism so as to distinguish it from *classical* Zionism, a term one would also encounter in the literature.[6] We shall explore the difference between these two Zionisms shortly. For now, it is important to know that *Zion* is a biblical name for Jerusalem or the ancient Land of Israel and political Zionism was and is, in essence, Jewish nationalism. It is the aspiration to establish a Jewish nation-state in Palestine and it emerged as a direct consequence of European antisemitism.

It is not well known that factions of European Christians also desired for Jews to settle in Palestine. This desire originated among certain circles in the aftermath of the 16th century Reformation and with an understanding of Bible passages carrying prescriptions to restore Jews to Palestine. Such Christian concern was not about the Jewish suffering in Europe, however. Rather, it was the belief that the settlement of Jews in Palestine was a precondition for the biblically promised Second Coming of the Messiah and the Christianization of the world. At the Coming, these Christians believed, Jews would either convert to Christianity or be condemned to hell.[7]

This understanding of biblical prophecy became prominent specifically in some of Britain's societal and political circles. There was, for example, the London Society for Promoting Christianity Among the Jews, the Society for the Investigation of Prophecy, and the British Society for the Propagation of the Gospel Among the Jews. As one 19th century observer commented, the building of Israel in Palestine is "favoured by some of the wisest, most learned, and best men in the Church of Christ."[8] That this popularity of Christian Zionism emerged in Britain was important because the country was among the great imperial powers of the day. It had the capabilities to accomplish the aspiration of Jewish settlement in Palestine.

However, such religious reasons to restore the Jewish people to Palestine, by themselves, did not drive British imperial policy. There would need to be a strategic reason and such emerged only later, that is, on the eve of the First World War. Christian religious motivations would come to play a supplementary role for Britain. Later on, these would become an important factor in the United States. Here too did factions of Christians see themselves called upon to restore Jews to Palestine. Also, these Christians were not concerned about the fate of Jews. Their motivation was the same as that just stated – the Second Coming and their personal salvation. The impact of these Christians on American favoritism toward Israel continues into the present and is very significant.

The Emergence of Political Zionism

The progress that had occurred in some parts of Europe in the first half of the 19th century was encouraging to many Jews. Many were eager to fully assimilate into European societies. Among the optimists was the Odessa physician Leo Pinsker. He had put his faith in the progress that the Jewish Emancipation and Enlightenment had brought. But in 1881, when he observed the horrific pogroms in his hometown, his thinking changed. Like Moses Hess before him, Pinsker concluded now that Jews would never be seen as equals in Europe.

Pinsker elaborated his thoughts in his book *Autoemancipation* (self-emancipation). Across Europe, he observed, there was repression and tyranny toward Jews, *Judeophobia*, as he called it. The ultimate solution to Judeophobia was *autoemancipation*, the reestablishment of the Jewish nation and the movement toward the building of a Jewish nation-state. At this time, Zionism, as a political program, was not officially formed yet, but Pinsker became the leader of *Hovevi Zion* (Lovers of Zion). This was a coalition of Jewish organizations from various countries and one of its foremost goals was to promote Jewish emigration to Palestine. Indeed, beginning in the early 1880s, the first European Jews started their journey to the Holy Land.

The pessimism of prominent Jews like Moses Hess and Leo Pinsker would soon be shared by Theodor Herzl whom we began this chapter with. Witnessing the Dreyfus Affair in Paris, it was manifest to Herzl that antisemitism was a serious problem for European Jews. Herzl, like

Hess and Pinsker, now also became convinced that for most Jews it was impossible to assimilate into European society. The problems that had long been confronting European Jews, the "Jewish Question" as it was often referred to, would continue to persist. This was a core argument in Herzl's famous 1896 book *Der Judenstaat* (The Jewish State). He wrote,

> The Jewish Question still exists. It would be foolish to deny it. It exists wherever Jews live in perceptible numbers. Where it does not yet exist, it will be brought by Jews in the course of their migrations. We naturally move to those places where we are not persecuted, and there our presence soon produces persecution. This is true in every country, and will remain true even in those most highly civilized – France itself is no exception – till the Jewish Question finds a solution on a political basis.[9]

The only solution to the Jewish Question, Herzl argued, was for Jews to build their own nation-state. Any difficulty toward this ambitious goal could be overcome, Herzl believed, because European leaders would help. Their societies were anti-Semitic, so they would welcome the Jews' departure and aid it. Herzl wrote,

> Let the sovereignty be granted [to] us over a portion of the globe large enough to satisfy the rightful requirements of a nation; the rest we shall manage for ourselves. The creation of a new State is neither ridiculous nor impossible. We have in our day witnessed the process in connection with nations which were not largely members of the middle class, but poorer, less educated, and consequently weaker than ourselves. The Governments of all countries scourged by anti-Semitism will be keenly interested in assisting us to obtain the sovereignty we want.[10]

Herzl was not quite sure yet where the Jewish state was to be. In the book he referred to both Palestine and Argentina as examples where "experiments in colonization" had taken place. What spoke for Argentina was that it had "vast open spaces." Palestine, however, as Herzl pointed out, was the Jews' "unforgettable homeland."[11] Before Herzl, other European Jews had argued for Jewish emigration to a new homeland. However, it was Herzl's *Der Judenstaat* that came to represent the most forceful articulation for a Jewish state. And it was also him who, in the following years, worked most ardently toward its realization.

It is important to note here that Herzl's political Zionism was, by far, not universally accepted among the European Jewry. Many Jews in

Western Europe maintained their desire to become fully integrated into European society. Others took issue with what they saw as a politicization of Judaism. A prominent critic was Asher Ginzberg, often known by his pen name Ahad HaAm. He was seen as the leader of what is sometimes referred to as *cultural Zionism*, and he and his followers saw Judaism as being defined by its spiritual dimensions. These, Ginzberg argued, would be corrupted by nationalism and the political ambition to build a state. Instead, the effort should be toward a spiritual center in Palestine, populated by Jews with a quest for learning and religious devotion.[12]

Regarding pious Jews in Europe, their life was often marked by what has sometimes been referred to as *classical* Zionism (as opposed to *political* Zionism). I alluded to this distinction earlier in this chapter. Similar to political Zionism, also in this understanding of Zionism there is a Jewish claim to Zion, that is, Jerusalem and the Holy Land. However, the charge for pious Jews anywhere was to remain patient and wait for God to bring forth the promised return. To pursue the reconstitution of a Jewish national home in Palestine through political means would be equal to a loss of faith in God's promise and was, therefore, to be rejected.[13]

The small Jewish minority that was living in Palestine at the end of the 19th century also did not support the ambitions of political Zionism. This minority is sometimes referred to as the Old Yishuv, meaning the long-standing Jewish communities in Palestine, and is to be distinguished from the New Yishuv, the Jewish communities that would be built from the early 1880s onward. The lives of the Old Yishuv were marked by traditionalism and rigorous religious practices which stood in contrast to the secular lives and political nation-state ambition that they observed among the European newcomers. Their reaction is well summarized by Daniel Gordis:

> The influx of European Zionists alarmed the Jews already living in Palestine, commonly known as the Old Yishuv. The Old Yishuv Jews were pious to the core and deeply loyal to their rabbinic authorities. To them, the new ideologically ultrasecular Yishuv seemed alien, even blasphemous.[14]

Despite reservations or even rejections of political Zionism among European and Palestinian Jews, Herzl's message did resonate, mostly among the Jews of Eastern Europe, many of whom lived in overt oppression and miserable poverty. Initially, it was for these Jews, more so than those living in Western Europe, for whom Theodor Herzl's vision provided a practical solution.

Herzl knew well that a book by itself would not be enough to achieve the goal of a Jewish state. What was needed was an institutional apparatus to coordinate activities while enhancing a Jewish national consciousness. Thus, only one year after publication of *Der Judenstaat*, Herzl moved to organize the First Zionist Congress. Held in August 1897 in the Swiss city of Basel, it was attended by an audience of more than 200, from about two dozen countries. After many hours of deliberation, its concluding program carried far-reaching ambitions. It stated, "The aim of Zionism is to create for the Jewish people a home in Palestine secured by public law."[15] Toward achieving this goal, the program specified four strategies:

1. The promotion, on suitable lines, of the colonization of Palestine by Jewish agricultural and industrial workers.
2. The organization and binding together of the whole of Jewry by means of appropriate institutions, local and international, in accordance with the laws of each country.
3. The strengthening and fostering of Jewish national sentiment and national consciousness.
4. Preparatory steps toward obtaining government consent, where necessary, to the attainment of the aim of Zionism.

The Congress also created a permanent association, namely the World Zionist Organization, which would hold regular meetings in the years to follow. Herzl was very pleased. In his diary he wrote, "At Basel I founded the Jewish State. If I said this out loud today, I would be answered by universal laughter. Perhaps in five years, and certainly in fifty, everyone will know it."[16] Indeed, exactly fifty years later the land of Palestine was about to be partitioned and fifty-one years later the Jewish State of Israel was founded.

As already mentioned, a Jewish state in Palestine would require the patronage of a European great power, but at this moment there was no support. Britain, which was generally sympathetic, offered Herzl an alternative possibility, namely Uganda in Africa. It was the year 1903 and the Kishinev pogrom (in today's Moldova) had just happened. To Herzl, this latest tragedy underlined the urgency for an immediate refuge. Wanting to give the British proposal serious consideration, at least as a temporary solution, he offered it for deliberation at the Sixth Zionist Congress that took place in the same year. It wasn't received too well; too many saw it as a betrayal of Zionism.[17] The refuge for the Jewish people had to be Palestine. That was the land to which they had a spiritual and emotional connection.

Theodor Herzl wouldn't be given more opportunities to work toward the establishment of a Jewish state. He died in 1904, at the young age of forty-four. He was buried in Vienna, but some decades later the World Zionist Organization decided that his proper resting place ought to be Jerusalem. In August 1949 he was reburied there, on a small hill, now called Mt. Herzl. After his death, the Zionist ambition for a Jewish state in Palestine continued. In fact, already in 1901, the Jewish National Fund (JNF) had been established with the purpose of raising funds and coordinating land purchases in Palestine.

First Experiences in Palestine

The first Jewish immigrants to Palestine came in the early 1880s. At this time, about 4 to 5 percent of Palestine's total population was Jewish. The new settlers saw themselves as *haluzim* (pioneers), and they had come as part of the first *Aliyah*, which began in 1882 and lasted until 1903. The term *Aliyah* means 'ascent,' and its use signaled that immigrating to the Holy Land was an act of elevation for Jews. By the end of the Aliyah, about 20,000–30,000 Jews had immigrated to Palestine.[18]

When Theodor Herzl was articulating his ideas about Jewish emigration to Palestine, he thought Jews would be welcomed because they would bring with them modernity and economic benefits to Arabs, for example through employment opportunities in new Jewish settlements. It would not come to such a harmonious situation. In their quest for a new homeland, European Zionists and settlers were dismissive not only of Palestinian nationalist ambitions that were growing at this time, but also of the Palestinian people generally. They often thought of Arabs as dishonest, lazy, primitive, and even barbarous.[19] One of the early settlers was Yitzhak Epstein, who in 1905, while the Zionist Congress met in Basel, made the following remarks at a meeting of a Hebrew cultural association:

> Among the difficult questions linked to the idea of rebirth of our people on its land, there is one question that outweighs all others: *the question of our attitude toward the Arabs.* This question, upon whose correct solution hangs the revival of our national hope, has not been *forgotten*, but has been completely *hidden* from the Zionists and in its true form is scarcely mentioned in the literature of our movement.[20]

But it wasn't just the settlers' arrogant attitudes that caused first tensions. The more significant issue was land purchases, or the "conquest of the land" as it is sometimes called in the literature.[21] These lands had been lived on and cultivated by Palestinian peasants and their families for decades and centuries, but during the Ottoman land reforms some decades earlier, these lands came to be owned by wealthy notables who often lived in faraway places. It was from them that the land was purchased, legally to be sure. The purchases were often financed by wealthy Europeans, like the French Baron Edmond de Rothschild, who then granted it to the settlers. As a result, the peasants, who for generations had worked the land, were driven off now, or were allowed to stay as a source of cheap labor. Even though these land purchases were very consequential to many Palestinian families, it should be noted that they did not amount to more than about 7 percent by the time Israel was founded in 1948.

The serious problems that the settlers' attitudes, combined with land purchases, would bring was foreseen early on by the aforementioned Asher Ginzberg. In an 1891 essay titled *The Truth from Eretz Yisrael* he wrote, "We who live abroad are accustomed to believing that the Arabs are all wild desert people who, like donkeys, neither see nor understand what is happening to them." "But this is a big mistake," he cautioned, and then warned, "[I]f the time comes when the life of our people in Eretz Yisrael develops to the point of encroaching upon the native population, they will not easily yield their place."[22] Indeed, tensions increased, and by the turn of the century, they were becoming harder to ignore.

By and large, however, the first Aliyah did not lead to significant changes in the lives of Palestinians. Matters would get worse, though, with the second Aliyah, beginning in 1904 and lasting until 1914. This new wave of immigrants included the twenty-year-old David Grün who arrived in 1906. A few years later, he hebraized his name to David Ben-Gurion, and he would come to be a uniquely significant figure in the creation of the State of Israel. Having experienced a wave of pogroms in Europe, Grün and many settlers in this second wave came with a firmer political commitment and a more assertive stance.

The settlers in this second Aliyah established the first political organizations and the first Jewish self-defense militia, which was named *HaShomer* (The Guard). The milita's motto is often cited in the literature as it is said to forecast coming conflict. It was, "By blood and fire Judea fell; by blood and fire Judea shall rise."[23] A central goal in the second Aliyah was that the conquest of land should now be accompanied by what was called the "conquest of labor."[24] Agricultural settlements and industrial plants were to operate more exclusively with Jewish workers. The Zionist goal, so it seemed, was to separate their economy from that of their Palestinian neighbors.

Palestinian resentments toward the new settlers grew as the years passed. The two Palestinian newspapers that were most outspoken in their criticism were *al Karmil* and *Filastin*. Notably, the editors of both papers were Christians. In 1910, *al Karmil* published translated passages from Herzl's *Der Judenstaat*. Its editor circulated a leaflet about Zionist goals in Palestine. It wasn't just immigration, he warned his fellow Arabs; it was an aim to take over Palestine. In 1914, *Filastin* wrote,

> Ten years ago the Jews were living as Ottoman brothers loved by all the Ottoman races ... living in the same quarters, their children going to the same schools. The Zionists put an end to all that and prevented any intermingling with the indigenous population. They boycotted the Arabic language and Arab merchants, and declared their intention of taking over the country from its inhabitants.[25]

Notably, the paper distinguished explicitly between Jews and Zionists. This distinction continues to be made by many Palestinians today. It is to emphasize that their quarrel is not with Jews or Judaism. Their quarrel, they say, was and is with political Zionism which, from the beginning, intended to take Palestinian lands away in order to build a Jewish nation-state.

The Issue of Settler Colonialism

In their search for territory where a Jewish homeland could be established, Zionists had considered places as diverse and distinct as Argentina, Uganda, South Africa, Cyprus, and the Sinai. Some of these considerations were rather fleeting, and some were deliberated more seriously. As we know, because of the Jewish religious connectedness to Palestine, it was ultimately there that Jews were to emigrate. And, as we have seen, this search for a new homeland was generated by surging antisemitism in Europe. It is this dire predicament of Jews in Europe that generated Zionism as a nationalist ideology. But Zionism, some scholars have argued, was also influenced by colonial ideas about white Europeans' self-assumed rights to claim and settle in other parts of the world.[26]

In making plans for a new home in Palestine, a Jewish state even, it was too often neglected that the land was home to its native population and that it had already used much of the farmable land. Zionists said that Palestine was largely an empty land, while it was, in fact, known that this was not true. At times, the falsity of Zionist propaganda was called out, as for example by Leo Motzkin, a delegate at the Second Zionist Congress. "In large stretches of land, one constantly comes across big Arab villages," he said, "and it is a well- established fact that the most fertile regions of our land are occupied by Arabs."[27]

A very similar acknowledgment was made by Elias Auerbach, who had been an active Zionist from his early youth. He grew up to be a prominent physician in Germany's Berlin and immigrated to Palestine in 1909, where he wrote historical essays. In a Zionist compendium from 1911 he wrote, "There are some simple truisms about Palestine ... The first of these truisms is that Palestine is not an empty land. The second is that the land takes its character from the predominant element in its population ... Palestine is an Arabic land." In order to make Palestine a Jewish land, Auerbach went on to say, "the Jews must become the principal element in the population."[28]

For Jews to establish themselves as a nation in Palestine, there had to be ongoing waves of mass immigration likely accompanied by the expulsion of the native population. In 1895, Herzl noted in his diary that it may well be necessary to "expropriate gently the private property on the state assigned to us" and "spirit the penniless population across the border by procuring employment for it in the transit countries, while denying it employment in our country." This had to happen without it being noticed. "Both the process of expropriation and the removal of the poor must be carried out discretely and circumspectly."[29]

Similar arguments were made by Israel Zangwill who was among Great Britain's prominent representatives of Jewish nationalism. At a 1905 Zionist meeting in Manchester he said, "[We] must be prepared either to drive out by the sword the [Arab] tribes in possession as our forefathers did or to grapple with the problem of a large alien population."[30] Some years later he wrote, "We cannot allow the Arabs to block so valuable a piece of historic reconstruction ... And therefore we must gently persuade them to 'trek.' After all, they have all Arabia with its million square miles ..."[31]

Based on observations like these, a growing number of scholars and observers argue that the Zionist movement was a settler colonialist movement.[32] What is settler colonialism? The term settler colonialism is best defined when differentiating it from classic colonialism. In the latter, the colonialists are not interested in building a new homeland or a state in the territory that they come to dominate. Instead, they desire the natural resources and the cheap labor of the land. The best-known example of this colonialism is perhaps the British domination in India. Settler colonialists, in contrast, as the term indicates, do want to settle on the new land and build a new homeland or a state.[33]

The settlers' initial impetus for this ambition of settling in a new place tends to be experiences of oppression at home. Thus, the desire for a new homeland is understandable. The fundamental problem, however, is that the new homeland is already inhabited by other people, the native population. Moreover, the settlers do not come as refugees to live alongside the natives; they come to live in their stead. Consequently, the native population has to be sufficiently marginalized, subdued in some way, or even done away with. This can occur through some cultural assimilation and integration of a small portion of the land's native inhabitants, but also through expulsion or genocide. The case of the U.S. is illustrative. The land, of course, had its natives, but these were not seen as equal upon the country's founding. Instead, they lived through generations of genocide and ethnic cleansing and were granted citizenship only in 1924.[34]

The goal of building a Jewish state also came at the expense of the land's native people, the Palestinians. Seeing Zionist immigration as a settler colonialist movement, scholars argue that it culminated with the establishment of Israel as a Jewish state in 1948. In the years since then, Israel is seen as a settler colonial state, having illegitimately taken possession of lands that belong to the Palestinians.[35] As observed by a critical scholar of Zionism:

> After all, the Zionists did not land in Jaffa port with the same intention harbored by persecuted Jews who landed in London or New York, that is, to live together in symbiosis with their new neighbors, the older inhabitants of their new surroundings. From the outset, the Zionists aspired to establish a sovereign Jewish state in the territory of Palestine, where the vast majority of the population was Arab. Under no circumstances could such a program of national settlement be completed without ultimately pushing a substantial portion of the local population out of the appropriated territory.[36]

As is to be expected, such views are rejected by much of the pro-Israel scholarship. These scholars emphasize that early Zionist leaders conceived of Zionism as a national liberation movement. It was a much-needed response to the dire Jewish predicament in Europe. They say that Jews were not coming to Palestine as foreign colonizers. Instead, they came as refugees to a land to which they had a spiritual connection. Moreover, they argue that Zionists did not aim at owning the entirety of Palestine as would be evidenced later on by their willingness to partition the land. That Israel came to be a state dominating all of Palestine, so the argument goes, was not the result of an existing intent of aggressive conquest but came in response to Arab attacks.[37]

As we have seen, it was indeed the case that there was a dire situation for Jews in Europe and there needed to be a solution to the so-called Jewish Question. The formulation of political Zionism was a seemingly necessary and legitimate answer. In this way, it was indeed a liberation movement for Jews living in poverty and oppression. However, to the extent that this liberation was connected to the colonization of a foreign land and the marginalization of its native people, it is highly problematic, of course.

Indeed, this is what seems to have happened. On the eve of the First World War, Moshe Sharett, who would later become Israel's first foreign minister, acknowledged, "We have forgotten that we have not come to an empty land to inherit it, but we have come to conquer a country from a people inhabiting it by virtue of its language and savage culture."[38] Some years later, David Ben-Gurion, Israel's first prime minister, acknowledged similarly, "[L]et us not ignore the truth among ourselves ... [P]olitically we are the aggressors and they defend themselves ... The country is theirs, because they inhabit it, whereas we want to come here and settle down ..."[39]

Conclusion

In this chapter, we went through a significant amount of background to the Israeli-Palestinian conflict. One of the important lessons is that the conflict was not generated in the Middle East, but in Europe. Poverty, discrimination, and violence made it difficult for Jews to remain there. They were looking for a new homeland, and thus Zionists came to make a claim to Palestine, a land that was already inhabited by its native Palestinians. As waves of Jews immigrated to Palestine, the first tensions and hostilities between native Palestinians and Jewish immigrants began. For many Palestinians, Jewish colonization of their land meant becoming dispossessed and displaced.

As the fronts were being set, questions of justice would emerge. This chapter is titled *A Conflict Made in Europe*. It is safe to say that without the long-running and horrific antisemitism in Europe, especially in the late 19th century, political Zionism may never have been born. For many decades now, Jews and Palestinians have been fighting each other, but the origins for the ongoing tragedy are squarely situated in Christian Europe. This is a fact that is rarely considered. Yet, it is important for anyone interested in the Israeli-Palestinian conflict to reckon with this argument because it is only through an understanding of historical roots that discussions about justice can be entertained.

Suggested Further Readings

Avineri, Shlomo. 1981. *The Making of Modern Zionism: The Intellectual Origins of the Jewish State*. New York: Basic Books.

Dowty, Alan. 2019. *Arabs and Jews in Ottoman Palestine*. Bloomington, IN: Indiana University Press.

Elon, Amos. 1983. *The Israelis: Founders and Sons*. New York: Penguin Books.

Khalidi, Rashid. 2009. *Palestinian Identity: The Construction of Modern National Consciousness*. New York: Columbia University Press.

Laquer, Walter. 1976. *A History of Zionism*. New York: Schocken Books.

Shafir, Gershon. 1996. *Land, Labor and the Origins of the Israeli-Palestinian Conflict, 1882–1914*. Berkeley, CA: University of California Press.

Shapira, Anita. 1999. *Land and Power: The Zionist Resort to Force, 1881–1948*. Stanford, CA: Stanford University Press.

Notes

1 Theodor Herzl. 1988. *The Jewish State*. New York: Dover Publications Inc., p. 96.
2 Mark Twain. 1899. Concerning the Jews. *Harper's Magazine* (September): 527–535 (quote is from p. 531).
3 For the elaboration of Jewish Emancipation and Enlightenment I am drawing from: Mark Tessler. 2009. *A History of the Israeli-Palestinian Conflict*. Bloomington, IN: Indiana University Press, pp. 26–36; Daniel Gordis. 2016. *Israel: A Concise History of a Nation Reborn*. New York: HarperCollins Publishers, pp. 13–14.
4 Quoted in Arthur Hertzberg. 1959. *The Zionist Idea: Historical Analysis and Reader*. New York: Anthenum, p. 121.
5 James Gelvin. 2014. *The Israel-Palestine Conflict*. Cambridge: Cambridge University Press, p. 43.
6 Mark Tessler, *A History of the Israeli-Palestinian Conflict*, pp. 16–24 and 43–53.
7 Shlomo Sand. 2012. *The Invention of the Land of Israel*. New York: Verso, pp. 119–175; Ilan Pappe. 2017. *Ten Myths About Israel*. New York: Verso, pp. 11–22.
8 Edward Swaine quoted in Eitan Bar-Yosef. 2003. "Christian Zionism and Victorian Culture." *Israel Studies* 8: 18–44 (quote is from p. 24).
9 Theodor Herzl, *The Jewish State*, p. 75.
10 Theodor Herzl, *The Jewish State*, p. 92.
11 Theodor Herzl, *The Jewish State*, p. 95.
12 Daniel Gordis, *Israel: A Concise History of a Nation Reborn*, pp. 54–57.
13 Mark Tessler, *A History of the Israeli-Palestinian Conflict*, pp. 16–20.
14 Daniel Gordis, *Israel: A Concise History of a Nation Reborn*, p. 70; see also: Mark Tessler, *A History of the Israeli-Palestinian Conflict*, p. 58.
15 Itamar Rabinovich and Jehufda Reinharz, eds. 2008. *Israel and the Middle East*, 2nd edition. Waltham, MA: Brandeis University Press, p. 21.
16 Theodor Herzl. 1960. *The Compete Diaries of Theodor Herzl*, edited by Rafael Patai, translated by Harry Zohn. New York: Herzl Press and Thomas Yoseloff, vol. 2. p. 581.

17 David Lesch. 2008. *The Arab-Israeli Conflict*. New York: Oxford University Press, p. 33.
18 David Lesch, *The Arab-Israeli Conflict*, pp. 28–29; James Gelvin, *The Israel-Palestine Conflict*, p. 56.
19 Benny Morris. 1999. *Righteous Victims*. New York: Alfred Knopf, p. 43.
20 Quoted in Alan Dowty. 2001. "'A Question that Outweighs All Others,' Yitzhak Epstein and Zionist Recognition of the Arab Issue." *Israel Studies* 6(1): 34–54 (quote is from p. 39; italics are in original).
21 Gershon Shafir. 1996. *Land, Labor and the Origins of the Israeli-Palestinian Conflict, 1982–1914*. Berkeley, CA: University of California Press.
22 The text of Ginzberg's essay as well as a critical appraisal of it can be found in Alan Dowty. 2000. "Much Ado about Little: Ahad Ha'am's 'Truth from Eretz Yisrael,' Zionism, and the Arabs." *Israel Studies* 5: 154–181.
23 Alan Dowty. 2019. *Arabs and Jews in Ottoman Palestine*. Bloomington, IN: Indiana University Press, p. 254.
24 Gershon Shafir, *Land, Labor and the Origins of the Israeli-Palestinian Conflict, 1982–1914*; Ian Black. 2017. *Enemies and Neighbors: Arabs and Jews in Palestine and Israel, 1917–2017*. New York: Atlantic Monthly Press, pp. 32–33; Ilan Pappe. 2004. *A History of Modern Palestine*. New York: Cambridge University Press, pp. 51–55.
25 Quoted in Alan Dowty, *Arabs and Jews in Ottoman Palestine*, p. 246.
26 Shlomo Sand, *The Invention of the Land of Israel*, p. 198; Ilan Pappe, *Ten Myths About Israel*, pp. 41–42.
27 Ian Black, *Enemies and Neighbors*, p. 26.
28 Quoted in Ian Black, *Enemies and Neighbors*, p. 32.
29 Theodor Herzl, *The Compete Diaries of Theodor Herzl*, vol. 1 p. 88.
30 Quoted in Meri-Jane Rochelson. 2010. *A Jew in the Public Arena: The Career of Israel Zangwill*. Detroit, MI: Wayne State University Press, p. 165.
31 Quoted in Benny Morris, *Righteous Victims*, p. 140.
32 Patrick Wolfe. 2006. "Settler Colonialism and the Logic of Elimination of the Native." *Journal of Genocide Research* 8(4): 387–409; Shlomo Sand, *The Invention of the Land of Israel*; Ilan Pappe. 2017. *The Biggest Prison on Earth*. London: Oneworld.
33 Ilan Pappe, *Ten Myths About Israel*, pp. 41–42.
34 Nadia Ben-Youssef and Samaan Tamari. 2018. "Enshrining Discrimination: Israel's Nation-State Law." *Journal of Palestine Studies* 48(1): . 73–74.
35 For critiques of this perspective see S. Ilan Troen. 2007. "De-judaizing the Homeland: Academic Politics in Rewriting the History of Palestine." *Israel Affairs* 13: 872–884.
36 Shlomo Sand, *The Invention of the Land of Israel*, p. 16.
37 Jacob Tsur. 1977. *Zionism: The Saga of a National Liberation Movement*. New Brunswick, NJ: Transaction; Connor Cruise O'Brien. 1986. *The Siege: The Saga of Israel and Zionism*. New York: Simon & Schuster.
38 Quoted in Benny Morris, *Righteous Victims*, p. 91.
39 Quoted in Simha Flapan. 1979. *Zionism and the Palestinians*. New York: Barnes and Noble Books, pp. 141–142.

3 The Holy Land Becomes the Embattled Land

Chaim Weizmann is a name that rings through much of the Israeli-Palestinian conflict's early history. He was born in 1874 in Russia to a traditional Jewish family. He attended a Jewish elementary school and became active in *Hovevi Zion* (Lovers of Zion) groups at a young age. Early on, he showed great talent for the study of the sciences. After finishing school, he departed from his home to pursue the study of chemistry, first in Berlin and then at Switzerland's University of Fribourg. During this time, Weizmann also attended the Second Zionist Congress in Basel and became increasingly active in the movement. After obtaining his doctorate degree, he moved to England, assuming a faculty position at the University of Manchester.

Weizmann was set for a most distinguished career. He proved himself to be an ingenious chemist and so his life would come to intersect in interesting ways with British imperial policy. In 1916, he was called to London to direct the British Admiralty laboratories and there he developed acetone, a substance that was very important for the British munitions industry. He came to be highly regarded and socialized in the capital's political circles, advancing himself to become the chief architect of a fateful British-Zionist alliance. Upon the founding of the State of Israel, he would serve as the country's first president.

Imperial Machinations in the Middle East

The First World War began in July 1914. Germany and Austria-Hungary were the Central Powers and were pitted against Russia, France, and Great Britain – the Allied Powers. In late October, the Ottoman Empire joined the Central Powers. In 1915, Italy joined the Allies and in 1917, the U.S. and Greece followed suit. Weizmann anticipated that the war would lead to the demise of the Ottoman Empire, which was ruling Palestine. He hoped that Britain would lay claim to the latter and that

DOI: 10.4324/9781003536260-3

British leaders would encourage a Jewish settlement there. This would not only help the ambition for a Jewish homeland, but, as Weizmann argued to British leaders, it would also bring civilization to the Middle East and be an effective guard for the British Suez Canal and British imperial interests more generally.[1]

Much before the outcome of the war was certain, there were already discussions among the Allies about the disposition of Ottoman territories in the Middle East. Russia wanted to have strategic access to the Mediterranean Sea, so it aimed for Istanbul and the Turkish Straits. France claimed rights in Syria and Lebanon. Britain was the world's dominant economic power and was adamant about its sea and land routes to India. It took the lead in initiating a series of conflicting promises and betrayals contained in three landmark documents: the McMahon–Hussein correspondence (1915–16), the Sykes–Picot Agreement (1915–16), and the Balfour Declaration (1917). The goal of all three documents was to establish imperial control in the Middle East.

The McMahon–Hussein Correspondence

In the years preceding the war, the Ottoman Empire was often caricatured as the "sick man of Europe," suggesting that its ultimate end was near. In fact, it still mustered a tremendous fighting capability, which the British and their allies came to experience in the famous 1915 Gallipoli campaign with which they aimed to take control of the Turkish straits and subsequently conquer Istanbul. The Ottomans fought back ferociously, prevailing against the Allied forces. Thus, they had to be defeated in another way, stimulating a consequential alliance between the British and some Arab leaders.

We encountered the 1789 French Revolution in Chapter 2. One of its effects was that nationalism spread across Europe. By the beginning of the 20th century, it also affected the Arab world where small groups banded together, demanding at first more autonomy but then also independence from the Ottoman Empire. Sharif Hussein bin Ali was the leader of this movement, and he bolstered his authority by virtue of being the guardian of Islam's two most sacred sites, namely Mecca and Medina, located in today's Saudi Arabia. The Sharif's ambition was to establish Arab independence from Syria in the north to Yemen in the south, and from the Mediterranean Sea in the west to Iraq in the east.

Toward this end, the Ottomans had to be ejected from Arab lands. But Hussein and his compatriots needed the help of a foreign power to do so. Given Britain's interests in the region, it was more than willing to take on this role. London leaders calculated that an Arab revolt in the

Ottoman's backyard would contribute to its ultimate fall. The British command center for the Middle Eastern war theater was in Cairo, Egypt, and the High Commissioner there was Sir Arthur Henry McMahon. It would be up to him to forge a pact between the British and the Arabs.

Thus, it came that between July 1915 and March 1916 Hussein bin Ali and Arthur McMahon exchanged a series of letters, known as the McMahon–Hussein correspondence. The most important letter in these exchanges was written by Hussein on September 9 where he demanded an agreement on the final boundaries for the future independent Arab state. McMahon responded on October 24, showing himself amenable to Hussein's desires, but adding one particular exclusion: "The two districts of Mersina and Alexandretta and portions of Syria lying to the west of the districts of Damascus, Homs, Hama and Aleppo cannot be said to be purely Arab, and should be excluded from the limits demanded."[2]

A look at Map 3.1 visualizes the situation for us. McMahon's demand is that present-day Lebanon would be excluded from the agreement. Palestine, however, would be part of the Arab state. Hussein was satisfied, not knowing that later on the British would resort to some twisted argument claiming that they, in fact, had meant to exclude Palestine from the agreement as well. Their argument was backed up by their power and, in due time, as Thucydides said, they would come to do what they had the power to do, namely claim Palestine.

For now, in the midst of the war's fighting, Hussein was provided with money, weaponry, and advisors, and he was ready to march. Supported by the British, in mid-1916, Arab contingents attacked Ottoman positions and soon captured various towns in the Hijaz, in today's Saudi Arabia. The campaign was going well, and the Arab rebels were looking forward to the realization of an independent Arabia. But all along the British had harbored very different plans for the Middle East.

The Sykes–Picot Agreement

While the British were negotiating with the Sharif about Arab independence, they were also negotiating with French leaders. Beginning at the end of 1915 and lasting until May 1916, Sir Mark Sykes for Britain and Francois Georges Picot for France were surveying maps of the Middle East as they forged an agreement over their countries' claims to Arab territories. The outcome was named after these two diplomats, the famous Sykes–Picot Agreement, a document that has caused Arab resentment until today.

According to the agreement illustrated in Map 3.2, Great Britain would obtain what would become Iraq, Transjordan, and the Negev

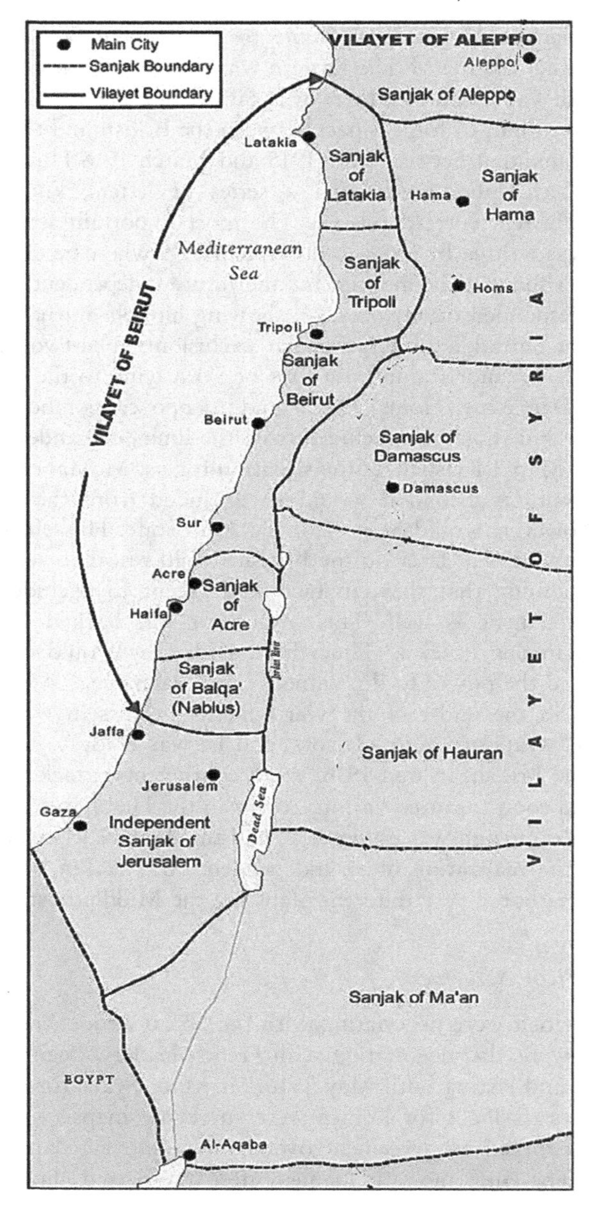

Map 3.1 Administrative Boundaries Under the Ottomans.
Source: Adapted version of a map from the Palestinian Academic Society for the Study of International Affairs, used with permission. The original map can be found at www.passia.org/maps/view/69

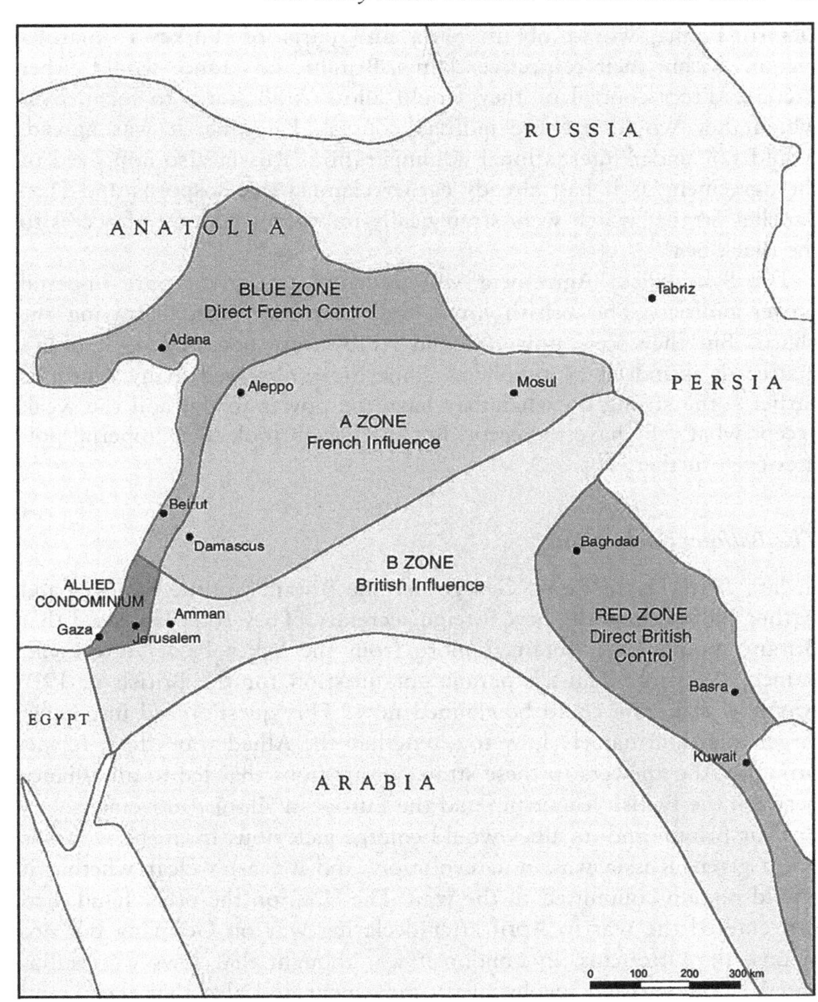

Map 3.2 The Sykes–Picot Agreement
Source: Adapted version of a map from the Palestinian Academic Society for the Study of International Affairs, used with permission. The original map can be found at www.passia.org/maps/view/4

Desert. France would obtain Syria and parts of Turkey's Anatolia region. Within their respective claims, Britain and France would either exercise direct control or they would allow Arab states to form, over which they would exercise indirect control. Palestine, it was agreed, would fall under international administration. Russia also approved of the agreement as it had already earlier claimed the Bosporus and Dardanelles Straits, which were strategically important because of access to the Black Sea.

The Sykes–Picot Agreement was a demonstration of pure imperial power politics. The British knew well that they were betraying the Sharif. But they were powerful and Arabs were not, and so it didn't matter. It is indeed as simple as Thucydides observed many centuries earlier – the strong do what they have the power to do, and the weak accept what they have to accept. But the British took their imperial politics even further.

The Balfour Declaration

In late 1916, David Lloyd George became Britain's prime minister and Arthur Balfour was the new foreign secretary. They soon lamented that Britain should have obtained more from the Sykes–Picot Agreement, namely Palestine. Thus, a paramount question for the British in 1917 was how Palestine could be claimed now. This question fed into a yet larger question, namely how to strengthen the Allied war effort. It was primarily the answers to these strategic questions that led to an alliance between the British leadership and the European Zionist movement.

That Britain and its allies would emerge victorious from the war was not a given. Russia was in a revolution, and it wasn't clear whether it would remain committed to the war. The U.S., on the other hand, had just entered the war in April after declaring war on Germany but not against the Ottomans. In London it was thought that Jews were influential in the Russian revolutionary movement and also that they could exert significant influence on President Wilson. Chaim Weizmann, whom we began this chapter with, did his part to strengthen such beliefs. Declaring British support for a Jewish national home, London leaders came to think, would motivate the Russian and American Jewry to exert their influence to keep Russia in the war and compel a widened American commitment.[3]

Great Britain itself also had very concrete interests in Palestine. Most importantly, as we saw previously, Palestine bordered Egypt and it was in the immediate vicinity to the Suez Canal, which was Britain's lifeline to India. Palestine, moreover, would allow for the building of a strategic corridor from the Mediterranean to Iraq and Iran, which would become increasingly important because of oil discoveries there. British leaders calculated that their help in establishing a Jewish homeland would indebt Palestine's new Jews to Great Britain, providing London with continued influence over a region that would only grow in its strategic relevance.

In addition to these material calculations, there was also the factor of Christian Zionism. As we saw in Chapter 2, it was a long-standing belief in British Protestant circles that the return of the Jews to Palestine would herald the Second Coming. Both Prime Minister Lloyd George and Foreign Secretary Arthur Balfour came from this faith tradition and were avid supporters of Zionism. Putting all these reasons together, on November 2, 1917, Foreign Secretary Balfour issued a public letter to Lord Lionel Walter Rothschild, who was a member of the House of Lords and the head of the British Zionist Organization. This was the famous Balfour Declaration shown in Figure 3.1.

While Jews were referred to as a "people," the native Palestinian majority were simply referred to as "non-Jewish communities." Palestinian Muslims constituted the vast majority of the population in Palestine and there were also Christian and Druze minorities, but they were all promised only "civil and religious rights." Nothing was said about their national rights and their rights to self-determination. Jews, by contrast, constituted less than 10 percent of the population in Palestine. Yet, they were ascribed national rights in Palestine. Finally, although the British promise was for a Jewish national home, and not a state, Chaim Weizmann was soon assured that what was really meant was an eventual Jewish state.[4]

British immorality knew no boundaries. In 1919, Arthur Balfour wrote the following to his successor Lord George Curzon:

> The contradiction between the letters of the Covenant and the policy of the Allies is … flagrant … [I]n Palestine we do not propose even to go through the form of consulting the wishes of the present inhabitants of the country … rooted in age-long traditions, in present needs, in future hopes, of far profounder import than the desires and prejudices of the 700,000 Arabs who now inhabit that ancient land. In short, so far as Palestine is concerned, the Powers have made no statement of fact which is not admittedly wrong, and no declaration of policy which, at least in the letter, they have not always intended to violate.[5]

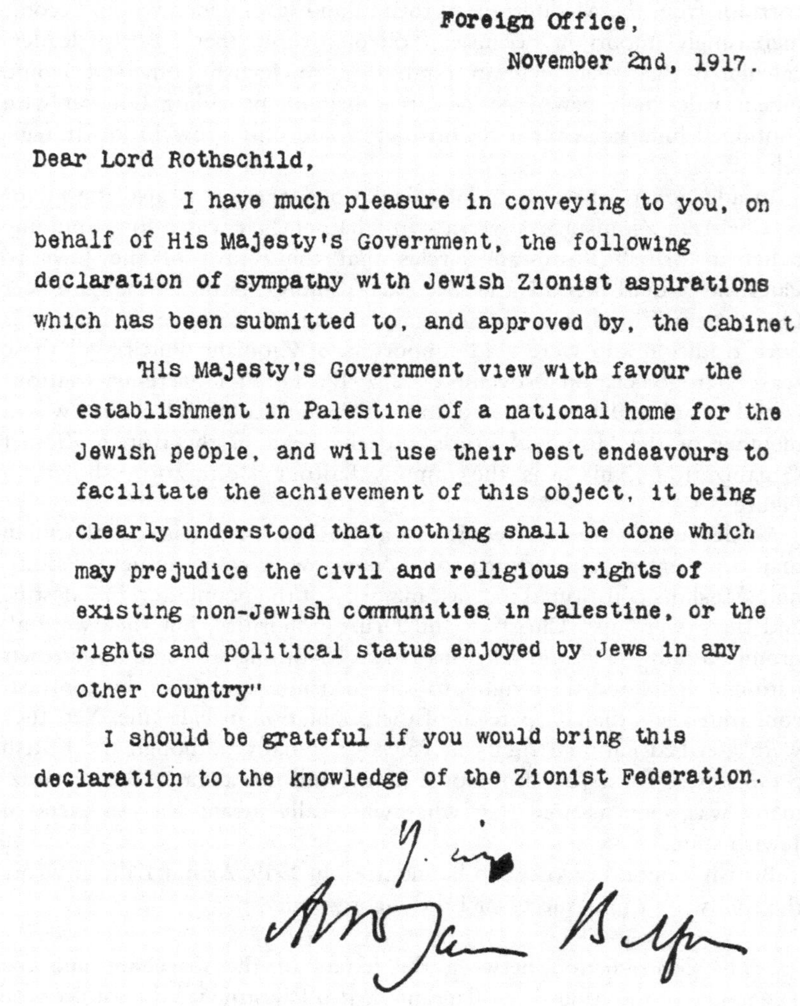

Foreign Office,
November 2nd, 1917.

Dear Lord Rothschild,

I have much pleasure in conveying to you, on behalf of His Majesty's Government, the following declaration of sympathy with Jewish Zionist aspirations which has been submitted to, and approved by, the Cabinet

"His Majesty's Government view with favour the establishment in Palestine of a national home for the Jewish people, and will use their best endeavours to facilitate the achievement of this object, it being clearly understood that nothing shall be done which may prejudice the civil and religious rights of existing non-Jewish communities in Palestine, or the rights and political status enjoyed by Jews in any other country"

I should be grateful if you would bring this declaration to the knowledge of the Zionist Federation.

Yours

Arthur James Balfour

Figure 3.1 The Balfour Declaration

The Balfour Declaration was a remarkable document of imperial arrogance. A European power made a promise about Palestinian lands to European people. For a third time in a short span, we see Thucydides' dictum at work; the strong do what they have the power to do, and the weak accept what they have to accept.

The War's Aftermath

In the fall of 1917, the British general Edmund Allenby marched his troops along the Mediterranean from Egypt toward Palestine. On December 11, the general entered Jerusalem and proclaimed victory. Less than one year later, in November 1918, Syria was also occupied and at the end of the month the Ottoman Empire conceded.

What would happen to Ottoman territories in the Middle East was to be ratified at the 1919 Paris Peace Conference and by the League of Nations, which would soon come into being. Encouraging to Palestinians was that President Woodrow Wilson appointed the King–Crane Commission, named after the Oberlin College president Henry King and the Chicago entrepreneur Charles Crane, to evaluate the situation in Palestine. Its investigations showed that the Zionist goal was to fundamentally transform Palestine. Indeed, for the occasion of the Paris conference, Chaim Weizmann presented a map that envisioned the Jewish homeland in all of Palestine.

It was clear that Zionist plans could come only at the price of grave injustices to the indigenous people, and the commission thus concluded that the Zionist ambitions in Palestine should be halted. Unfortunately for Palestinians, the report didn't have any impact. Although appointed by Wilson, the president himself was very attracted to the idea of the Jewish people being reborn in the Holy Land. Zionist lobbying in Washington had also started by this time, and in 1922, U.S. lawmakers approved a declaration in support of the Balfour Declaration.

The ultimate fate for former Ottoman lands was left to the April 1920 San Remo Conference in Italy. The Allied powers agreed to divide the lands into so-called mandates. In these mandates, the native people had only limited political power over their own communities; real authority rested with a foreign mandatory power. Once the indigenous people would be judged to have matured sufficiently so as to govern themselves, the mandate would terminate.

Britain was granted the mandate for what would become Iraq, Transjordan, and Palestine. France obtained the mandate for what would become Syria and Lebanon. In July 1922, the League of Nations Council confirmed the Palestinian mandate. It was official now that Arabs had been betrayed in their quest for independence. In a move to calm Arab anger, Britain allowed Hussein's son Faisal to become king in Iraq and his older brother, Abdullah, to become king in Transjordan. Both countries were ruled under British authority but acquired independence in 1932 and 1946, respectively.

In its ratification of the Palestine mandate, the League of Nations also included the Balfour Declaration in the preamble. Toward the end of a Jewish homeland, the Jewish Agency would come to function as a quasi-government. It was supported not only by the British government, but also by the financial aid of wealthy American and European Jews. In the years to come, the Agency was engaged in institution building in realms such as labor, health, and education, and it also represented Jewish interests in Palestine to British authorities.[6] Further institution building came with the establishment of the Haganah, a defense organization initiated in response to some violence between Jewish immigrants and native Palestinians. Britain provided training, arms, and organizational support.

Palestinian institutions could not match the Yishuv's. The Arab Executive and the Supreme Muslim Council were founded in the early 1920s, but both proved weak vehicles for Palestinian aspirations in good part because the British saw to it that they had little unity. Palestinian life had long been governed by notable families, most significantly the al-Husseinis and the Nashashibis, and their relationship was often competitive. In 1921, the British High Commissioner Sir Herbert Samuel chose Amin al-Husseini from the al-Husseini family to be the Grand Mufti of Jerusalem and to head the Supreme Muslim Council. Both were important positions, but the appointment came against the recommendation of a Muslim selection committee and it thus furthered the division in the Palestinian leadership.

The Palestinian leadership has also been alleged to have had a lack of pragmatism. For example, Palestinian leaders rejected Samuel's proposal to create a legislative council that would be comprised of elected and appointed Christian, Jewish, and Muslim delegates. While there was indeed Palestinian rigidity at times, it is also important to consider their view here. Palestinians constituted the vast majority of the population and, from their perspective, they could simply not accept the Zionist insistence on equal representation in any council, nor could they accept British authority in Palestine. Accepting any such arrangement would legitimize expansionist Zionist ambitions as well as the mandate itself.[7]

The Iron Wall

As we have seen, within the Zionist movement there was the ambition to convert all of Palestine into a Jewish state. It was only to be expected that it would come to confrontational resistance. On the Zionist side, this anticipation was acknowledged forthrightly by the Zionist leader Ze'ev Jabotinsky in his often-cited 1923 essay *The Iron Wall*. "Every native population in the world," he wrote, "resists colonists as long as it has the slightest hope of being able to rid itself of the danger of being colonized. That is what the Arabs in Palestine are doing, and what they will persist in doing as long as there remains a solitary spark of hope that they will be able to prevent the transformation of 'Palestine' into the 'Land of Israel'."[8]

In 1925, Jabotinsky founded the Revisionist Party, which was named so because it wanted to revise the terms of the British Mandate. According to Revisionists, Transjordan was to be part of Palestine and of the future Jewish state. Regardless of how far the Land of Israel would ultimately extend, the anticipated resistance necessitated an Iron Wall, that is a preponderant power advantage over Palestinians and neighboring Arabs. Through this wall, Jabotinsky argued, any Arab would come to realize that their resistance is futile. It is at that moment that there could be a settlement with the Arabs, but it would happen only after colonization had taken place. At first, according to Jabotinsky, Zionists would have to rely on a foreign power to establish the Iron Wall.[9]

It did not take long for the Yishuv leaders to embrace Jabotinsky's Iron Wall strategy. Great Britain was, of course, the foreign power under which Zionist colonization first proceeded. Later on, after the Second World War, and especially after the 1967 War, the U.S. was the foreign power under which Zionist ambitions proceeded yet further. The Yishuv and then Israel indeed developed quickly into by far the most powerful state in the region, in fact, the only nuclear power in the region. With that power, to paraphrase Thucydides, Israel came to do what it had the power to do.

An Intensifying Conflict

The anticipated resistance was already underway. During the Paris Peace Conference, the third Aliyah had begun. It lasted until 1923, and brought about 35,000 Jewish immigrants to Palestine. Beginning in the spring of 1920, Palestinian attacks on Jews became more frequent and a particularly ferocious incident occurred in May 1921 when a Jaffa hostel was attacked, resulting in over a dozen Jewish fatalities. The violence spread beyond Jaffa and, over nearly a week of violence, it came to dozens of casualties on both sides. The British charged the Haycraft Commission, named after its chairperson, the Chief Justice of Palestine Sir Thomas Haycraft, to examine the causes for the violence. Its resulting account put the blame on the Palestinians, but it also pointed to their legitimate political and economic fears resulting from continuous Jewish immigration.[10]

One year after the Jaffa violence, the British issued a so-called white paper, a statement of intended policy. With it, the British hoped to cater to both communities and calm the tensions. Jews were assured that they are in Palestine "as of right, and not on sufferance." Palestinians were promised that there was no intention to convert all of Palestine into a Jewish national home and that there would be limitations to Jewish immigration.[11] In the end, neither community was placated. Jews felt betrayed and Arabs continued to feel imposed on as a foreign power decided over their land. Despite the intent of limiting immigration, the fourth Aliyah, which began in 1924 and ended in 1928, brought about 80,000 immigrants, more than twice the number of the preceding Aliyah.

As this most recent wave of immigration came to an end, the conflict took a religious dimension at Jerusalem's Western Wall. The escalation began already a year prior, when Jews and Muslims were quarreling over access to and control of the Temple Mont/Haram al-Sharif and over the Western Wall specifically. Over the course of a year matters got worse, and in mid-August 1929, there were Jewish demonstrations and Muslim counter-protests. These, in turn, escalated into violence and quickly spread beyond Jerusalem to the cities of Hebron, Jaffa, and Safad. The worst atrocities occurred in Hebron with nearly sixty casualties. Altogether over 130 Jews were killed, mostly by Palestinians. On the Palestinian side, more than 100 were killed, mostly by British soldiers and police.[12]

The British again formed a commission to investigate the causes of the violence. It was the Shaw Commission, named after the distinguished British lawyer Sir Walter Shaw. Palestinians were to be blamed, the commission concluded. However, like the Haycraft Commission a few years prior, this commission also contextualized the assaults, stating the violence had its roots in Palestinians' disappointment over their national and political ambitions as well as the increasing number of land transfers and evictions they were experiencing. It also repeated the earlier recommendation of the Haycraft Commission to put restrictions on Jewish mass immigration.[13]

The Rise of Hitler in Germany

At this point, it is important to pause our discussion of the situation in Palestine and direct attention to happenings in Europe. In 1933, Adolf Hitler took power in Germany and from that year onward there would be continuous Nazi campaigns of Jewish oppression. In 1935, the infamous Nuremberg Laws were adopted, stripping Jews of citizenship and imposing other repressive restrictions. In 1938, the infamous *Reichskristallnacht* (night of broken glass) took place, involving the destruction of Jewish synagogues, stores, and other buildings, and resulting in many casualties.

The Nuremberg Laws and the Reichskristallnacht are only two examples of the horror that Jews were living through and, naturally, many wanted to leave. A favored destination for most Jews, so far, had been the U.S. But there, Jews had become increasingly unwanted and the U.S. began initiating immigration restrictions. Britain took a similar stance and the destination for many Jews now became Palestine. The fifth Aliyah began in about 1929 and would last until about 1939. With well over 200,000 newcomers, it was larger than any of the preceding immigration waves. In the few years between 1931 and 1936 the Jewish population in Palestine more than doubled, now constituting nearly 30 percent of the overall population.[14] A demographic shift in Palestine in favor of a Jewish majority seemed to become a possibility.

Militarization of the Conflict

With increased immigration, the situation in Palestine was intensifying. The Haganah had been the main defense organization for the Yishuv since 1920. But by 1931 a group of its officers saw it as too restrained. They formed their own military arm, the *Irgun Tzvai Leumi* (National Military Organization), and in the coming years it would align itself with Jabotinsky's revisionist movement. Overall, the Yishuv's strength increased through the number of fighters and also in weaponry. The Haganah was developing its own arms and munition factories, and it was continuing to smuggle weapons from Europe. When in October 1935 a large shipment of weapons and ammunition was discovered in the port of Jaffa, the warning for Palestinians seemed clear: The Yishuv were mobilizing for war.[15]

Palestinians also formed their guerilla organizations. The best known was *al-Kaff al-Aswad* (the Black Hand), led by Sheikh Izzedin al-Qassam, a religious leader from Haifa. Possibly it was the Jaffa discovery that motivated him and his band to a renewed escalation, beginning with the murder of a Jewish police officer in early November. When British forces pursued and killed al-Qassam, he was widely seen as a martyr. His funeral became a nationalist demonstration, initiating mass resistance and an escalation of vengeful violence. In mid-April 1936, for example, Palestinians murdered three Jews near Nabulus. It was followed by counter murders and mutual attacks, and the situation was about to spiral out of control.[16]

Amid the unfolding chaos, various political parties, notable families and groups, Muslims and Christians came together to form the Arab Higher Committee (AHC). Led by the Mufti Amin al-Husseini, it was a renewed attempt to unify the Palestinian national movement. Marking the beginning of what would come to be known as the Arab Revolt, in the spring of 1936, the Committee declared a national strike and called for acts of civil disobedience as it demanded an end to both Jewish immigration and land sales to Jews, as well as the formal recognition of a Palestinian government. The strikes were soon accompanied by violence directed at British security positions but also at civilian institutions and settlements.

Once again, the Mandate was experiencing serious ruptures, and once again the British government formed a commission to determine the causes and a path forward. Named after its chairperson William Peel, the commission began its investigations in late 1936 and produced its report by the following summer. Its main conclusion can be summarized quickly: The Mandate was not workable. In one of its most quoted lines, the report stated, "An irrepressible conflict has arisen between two national communities within the bounds of one small country ... There is no common ground between them."[17]

Given this grim diagnosis, what was the prescription? According to the commissioners, it was the partitioning of Palestine. The plan, as shown in Map 3.3, was that a Jewish state would come to be on about 20 percent of the Mandate. It was to be comparatively small, but it was significantly more than the roughly 6 to 7 percent of land the Jews actually owned in Palestine. Moreover, it was the Mandate's best and most fertile land. The Palestinian state would come to be in the eastern mountains and the Negev Desert. A corridor stretching from the Mediterranean to Jerusalem would remain under British rule.

Both the Jewish Agency Executive and the Arab Higher Committee were to consider the plan. Zionist leaders lamented the small size, but David Ben-Gurion, who, in the meantime, had assumed the chairmanship of the Executive, advocated for it to be accepted. Acceptance was tactically necessary, Ben-Gurion argued, and once a strong Jewish state was established, he reasoned, it could be the springboard toward further expansion.[18] While expanding the Jewish territories, a Jewish majority had to be ensured, either through the transfer of Palestinians or through their expulsion. In a letter from October 1937 to his son he wrote,

> We must expel Arabs and take their places ... and, if we have to use force – not to dispossess the Arabs of the Negev and Transjordan, but to guarantee our own right to settle in those places – then we have force at our disposal.[19]

With Ben-Gurion's advocacy, and with an urgent need to provide a safe haven for Europe's Jews, the Zionist elite agreed to the Peel plan.[20] To

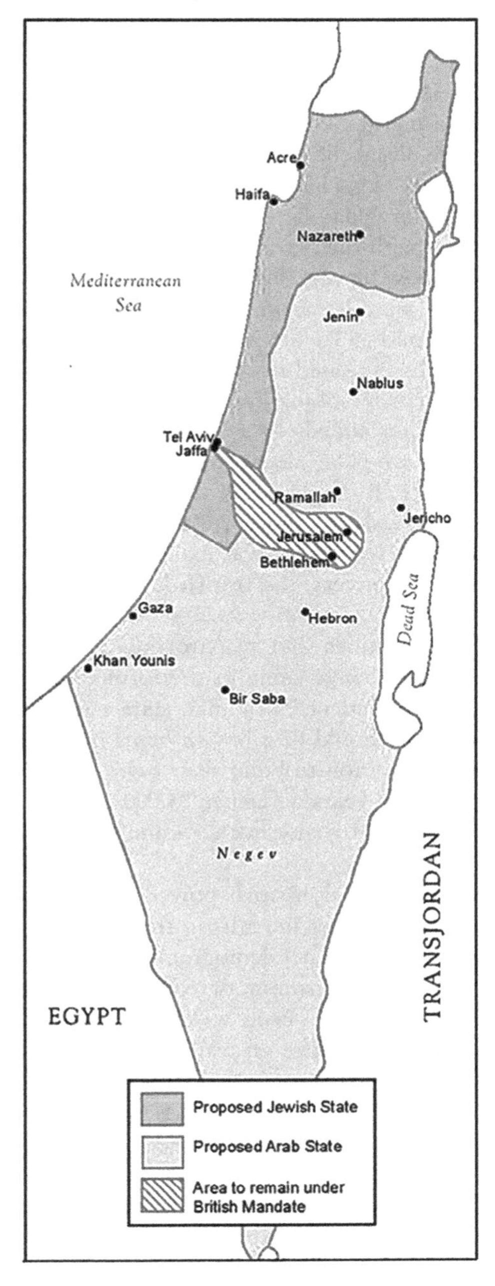

Map 3.3 The Peel Partition Plan
Source: Adapted version of a map from the Palestinian Academic Society for the Study of International Affairs, used with permission. The original map can be found at www.passia.org/maps/view/8

Palestinians, on the other hand, it was just not acceptable that the British could simply partition their land for the benefit of foreign immigrants. Thus, without any settlement in sight, the Arab Revolt continued. When in September 1937 a high-ranking British official was murdered in Nazareth, the British made illegal the Arab Higher Committee and had many of its leaders arrested. Al-Husseini escaped, first to Lebanon, then to Iraq, and eventually to Berlin where he would disgrace himself as he sought to make common cause with the Nazis against the British and the Jews.

The revolt was now in the hands of local leaders. About 10,000 Palestinian guerrillas were launching attacks on both British and Jewish targets. Until about mid-1937, the Yisuhuv had exercised themselves in restraint. But as Arabs escalated the fight, the Irgun started carrying out its own terrorist attacks, bombing, for example, Arab markets and cafes, with dozens of civilians killed. In response, the British brought their preponderant power to play, deploying some 25,000 servicemen and squadrons of bombers. By early 1939, they defeated the revolt. About 5,000 Palestinians were dead, about 2,000 homes were destroyed, and much of the Palestinian leadership was exiled.[21]

Despite this military success, the British leadership now fully realized that its commitment to Zionism was a serious liability causing confrontations with Arab states and jeopardizing British interests in the region. A fundamental change came in the form of a new white paper that envisioned an independent Palestinian state within ten years. While it maintained that there should be a Jewish *home* in a Palestinian state, it rejected any Zionist ambition to build their own *state*. According to the paper, over the next five years a further 75,000 Jews would be allowed into Palestine, but afterwards any further immigration would be subject to Arab consent.

Since the First World War, British power and support for Zionism had changed Palestine. It was unrealistic that it would ever return to the state it had been in. The demographic realities were different now, and these had to be accommodated. In this light, it seems, the 1939 white paper should have been welcomed by the Palestinian leadership as it did recognize their grievances and offered to build their own state. However, while most Palestinians were reportedly in favor of the plan, the reconstituted Arab Higher Committee came to stand against it.[22] Later on, the Palestinian rejection came to be seen by many as a historic blunder, as it squandered the best offer Palestinians would ever receive to build their own state. On the other hand, it should also be stated that the AHC had good reason to distrust the British and the Zionist ambitions and that partition of the homeland was just principally not an option.

Zionists, for their part, were outraged by the white paper. "Satan himself could not have created a more distressing and horrible nightmare," Ben-Gurion noted in his diary.[23] It only strengthened their ambition to claim Palestine, as was evidenced by what would become an often-referenced conference at New York's Biltmore Hotel in May 1942. It was attended by American and European Zionist leaders and also by David Ben-Gurion and Chaim Weizmann. The conclusions, known as the Biltmore Program, called for the establishment of a Jewish state in all of Palestine. Such, however, would create the demographic issue of too many Arabs in the Jewish state, a problem that has challenged Jewish leaders until today.[24]

Indeed, the white paper caused significant radicalization among the Yishuv. Already in the wake of the Arab Revolt did the Haganah move from a posture of defense to offensive maneuvers. In 1944, the Irgun came to be led by Menachem Begin, a future prime minister of Israel. Out of the Irgun, the *Lohamei Herut Israel* (Fighters for the Freedom of Israel), in short *Lehi*, would form, and also in this group there was a future Israeli prime minister, Yitzhak Shamir. The Lehi was so scrupulous that it even sought to collaborate with Nazis against the British.[25] Both groups aimed at securing the whole of Palestine for Jews. The immediate goal for now, however, was to drive the British out.

Among the Haganah's deeds were the destruction of railways and roads. The Irgun assaulted British army camps and destroyed vehicles, planes, and shops. The Lehi, after launching several unsuccessful attempts to assassinate the British High Commissioner Harold MacMichael, did succeed in murdering Lord Moyne, Britain's Secretary of State for the colonies and the Middle East's highest-ranking British official. One of the most horrific attacks occurred in the summer of 1946 when the Irgun bombed Jerusalem's King David Hotel, which had served as headquarters of the British civil and military administration. The act killed over ninety people, nearly a third of whom were Jews. The situation was becoming unbearable for Britain.

The Road to Partitioning Palestine

The Second World War seriously battered Britain and it would be unable to maintain its historical imperial ambitions. In its stead, the U.S. advanced as the preeminent power on the world stage. In 1942, U.S. troops arrived in North Africa, beginning its permanent presence in the region. Starting with the Biltmore Conference, the U.S. also took more of a role in Palestine's future. The number of Zionist associations increased and pro-Zionist Christian groups were also formed. There were intensive fundraising and advertising campaigns for a Jewish state, and politicians, including President Roosevelt, were lobbied toward this goal. In 1944, both chambers of Congress proposed resolutions for Jewish immigration to Palestine and both parties adopted pro-Zionist positions in their programs.[26]

When President Roosevelt died in April 1945, Harry Truman succeeded him. Despite the State Department's warnings that supporting Zionist ambitions would alienate the Arab world and potentially imperil U.S. interests in the Middle East, Truman proved to be a strong supporter of a Jewish state. Historians have put forward a list of factors to explain this. These include his own biblical beliefs in the Jews' restoration to Palestine as well as a humanitarian concern for the disaster that had befallen the Jews during the war. There was, furthermore, the pressure from domestic lobbying groups and the economic and political clout the American Jewry was said to have in congressional and presidential elections. Last but not least, there was also the strategic goal of not allowing a future Jewish state to become a Soviet ally.[27]

In February 1947, the British announced that it would submit Palestine's fate to the United Nations. The international organization established a Special Committee on Palestine (UNSCOP) to prepare proposals for Palestine's future. Both the Arab Higher Committee and the Arab League, a loose group of Arab states, rejected the idea that the UN would have any authority over Palestine and refused to cooperate with UNSCOP. The Committee proceeded nevertheless and concluded its work by outlining three possible scenarios: a unitary state with safeguards for minorities, a unitary bi-national state, or partition into two states. While a few states stressed that partition would violate the Palestinian right to self-determination and thus recommended a unitary state, the majority of the committee concluded that two states was the better choice.[28]

The UN General Assembly vote was scheduled for the end of November. In the days prior to the final vote, there were indications that the proposed partition might fail to reach the necessary two-thirds majority. Zionists consequently embarked upon an intensive lobbying campaign on the U.S, with the goal that the latter would pressure weaker governments to vote for partition. The strategy worked. It was November 29, and Resolution 181, often referred to as the partition resolution, passed narrowly with thirty-three voting in favor, thirteen against, and ten abstentions.[29]Map 3.4 illustrates the partition plan.

At a time when Jews were just about one third of Palestine's population and owned a mere 6 or 7 percent of the land, the new Jewish state

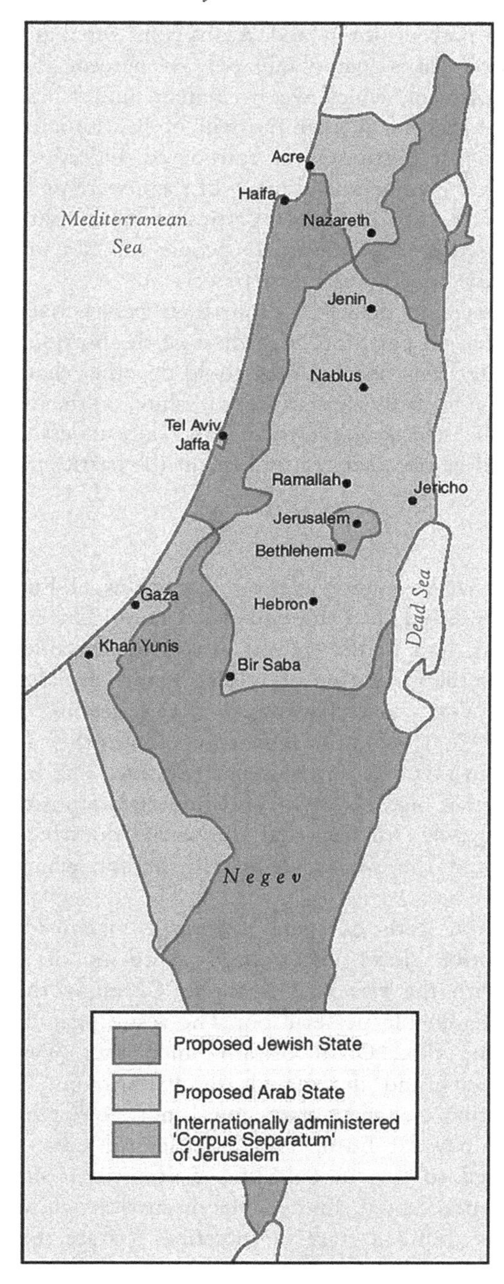

Map 3.4 The United Nations Partition Plan
Source: Adapted version of a map from the Palestinian Academic Society for the Study of International Affairs, used with permission. The original map can be found at www.passia.org/maps/view/15

would obtain 55 percent of the land. Arabs constituted almost two thirds of the population but would obtain only 44 percent. The remaining 1 percent was Jerusalem, which was to remain under international rule. Throughout the process, neither the will of Palestinians nor the UN's authority to propose partition was considered. Indeed, at the time, the UN had only sixty members, and many of them were under the influence of the U.S. and the Soviet Union. Critics of the resolution argue that what was imposed on the Palestinian people was not international law but the will of the world's strongest powers.

Palestinians were in disbelief. From their perspective, as the land's native population, no partition, regardless of the portion sizes, could be justified. But there was nothing they could do other than to declare the partition decision to be illegitimate. The Yishuv, on the other hand, were celebrating in the streets, while their leadership understood right away that force would be necessary to implement the partition.

Conclusion

In this chapter we saw how imperial ambitions of European powers turned the Holy Land into the embattled land. The British were the Yishuv's patron, and British power was indispensable in laying the groundwork for the formation of a Jewish state in Palestine. With the Second World War, the U.S. came to take a leading role in Middle East, and in 1947, it was crucial in compelling other states to pass a UN resolution in favor of partitioning Palestine. The history reviewed here is, in short, a history of forceful imperial imposition. It is illustrative of Thucydides' dictum that the strong do what they have the power to do and the weak, ultimately, accept what they have to accept.

This conclusion leads us again to engage in considerations about matters of justice. Jews experienced centuries of persecution in Europe, and with the rise of Nazism in Germany they became the victims of unimaginable persecution. The resulting refugee crisis was massive, but the U.S., Great Britain, and other Western countries closed their doors and designated the Palestinians' land for these refugees. Palestinians, of course, could not comprehend why they should have to pay for Europeans' cruelties to Jews. If Jewish refugees just wanted to live in Palestine, Palestinians often argue, that would have been accepted. But, as our discussions show, they wanted more, namely to build a state in Palestine, a state that would come with the disempowerment and dispossession of Palestinians in their own land.

Suggested Further Readings

Antonius, George. 1965. *The Arab Awakening*. New York: Capricorn Books.

Cohen, Michael. 1987. *The Origins and Evolution of the Arab-Zionist Conflict*. Berkeley, CA: University of California Press.

Darwin, John. 1981. *Britain, Egypt, and the Middle East: Imperial Policy in the Aftermath of War, 1918–1922*. London: Palgrave Macmillan.

Friedman, Isiah. 1973. *The Question of Palestine: British-Jewish-Arab Relations*. London: Routledge and Kegan Paul.

Segev, Tom. 2001. *One Palestine, Complete: Jews and Arabs Under the British Mandate*. New York: Metropolitan Books.

Segev, Tom. 2019. *A State at Any Cost: The Life of David Ben-Gurion*. New York: Farrar, Straus and Giroux.

Notes

1 Chaim Weizmann. 1949. *Trial and Error: The Autobiography of Chaim Weizmann*. New York: Harper and Brothers, p. 149.
2 Walter Laquer and Barry Rubin, eds. 2008. *The Israel-Arab Reader*, 7th edition. New York: Penguin Books, p. 11.
3 Jonathan Schneer. 2010. *The Balfour Declaration: The Origins of the Arab-Israeli Conflict*. New York: Random House.
4 Rashid Khalidi. 2020. *The Hundred Years' War on Palestine*. New York: Metropolitan Books, p. 25.
5 UN Committee on the Exercise of the Inalienable Rights of the Palestinian People (CEIRPP). 1990. *The Origins and Evolution of the Palestine Problem: 1917–1988*. Available at www.un.org/unispal/document/auto-insert-199840/
6 Mark Tessler. 2009. *A History of the Israeli-Palestinian* Conflict. Bloomington, IN: Indiana University Press, p. 194.
7 David Lesch. 2008. *The Arab-Israeli Conflict*. New York: Oxford University Press, p. 95; Benny Morris. 1999. *Righteous Victims*. New York: Alfred Knopf, p. 109.
8 The essay is available at http://en.jabotinsky.org/media/9747/the-iron-wall.pdf
9 Avi Shlaim. 2014. *The Iron Wall*. New York: W.W. Norton & Company, pp. 11–17.
10 Mark Tessler, *A History of the Israeli-Palestinian Conflict*, pp. 171–172.
11 Michael Cohen. 1987. *The Origins and Evolution of the Arab-Zionist Conflict*. Berkeley, CA: University of California Press, p. 82.
12 Alex Winder. 2012. "The 'Western Wall' Riots of 1929." *Journal of Palestine Studies* 42: 6–23; Mark Tessler, *A History of the Israeli-Palestinian Conflict*, p. 236; Ian Black. 2017. *Enemies and Neighbors: Arabs and Jews in Palestine and Israel, 1917–2017*. New York: Atlantic Monthly Press, pp. 56–64; David Lesch, *The Arab-Israeli Conflict*, pp. 105–106.
13 Charles Smith. 2004. *Palestine and the Arab-Israeli Conflict*, 5th edition. New York: Bedford/St. Martin's, p. 127.
14 Justin McCarthy. 1990. *The Population of Palestine*. New York: Columbia University Press, pp. 35–36.

15 Gudrun Krämer. 2008. *A History of Palestine*. Princeton, NJ: Princeton University Press, p. 263; Mark Tessler, *A History of the Israeli-Palestinian Conflict*, p. 231.
16 Ian Black, *Enemies and Neighbors*, p. 74.
17 The full report of the Peel Commission is available at https://ecf.org.il/media_items/290
18 Simha Flapan. 1987. *The Birth of Israel*. New York: Pantheon Books, p. 22.
19 Quoted in Shabati Teveth. 1985. *Ben-Gurion and the Palestinian Arabs*. Oxford: Oxford University Press, p. 189.
20 Benny Morris. 1999. *Righteous Victims*, p. 143.
21 Benny Morris, *Righteous Victims*, pp. 147 and 159–160; Ian Black, *Enemies and Neighbors*, p. 83; Noura Erakat. 2019. *Justice for Some*. Stanford, CA: Stanford University Press, p. 42; Rashid Khalidi, *The Hundred Years' War on Palestine*, p. 44.
22 Benny Morris, *Righteous Victims*, p. 158; Ian Black, *Enemies and Neighbors*, p. 90.
23 Tom Segev. 2001. *One Palestine Complete*. New York: Metropolitan Books, pp. 440–441.
24 Benny Morris, *Righteous Victims*, pp. 168–169.
25 Benny Morris. 2008. *1948: The First Arab-Israeli War*. New Haven, CT: Yale University Press, p. 29.
26 David Lesch, *The Arab-Israeli Conflict*, pp. 129–130; Benny Morris, *Righteous Victims*, p. 171.
27 David Lesch, *The Arab-Israeli Conflict*, p. 132.
28 Noura Erakat, *Justice for Some*, p. 45.
29 Michael Cohen, *The Origins and Evolution of the Arab-Zionist Conflict*, pp. 126–127.

4 The Wars Begin

Gamal Abdel Nasser was born in 1918 in Egypt's northern port city of Alexandria. At a time when the British were engaging in plentiful imperial machinations across the region, his family carried a strong sense of dignity and glory. Already in his teenage years did Nasser feel offended by his country's subservience to Europe, leading him to participate in protests against British colonialism. In 1937, he entered the Royal Military Academy in Cairo and met with other like-minded cadets. Eventually, they would come to be known as the Free Officers.

In the meantime, the British demonstrated their hold on Egypt when, in 1942, they surrounded Cairo's Abdeen Palace with tanks and troops and forced King Farouk to appoint a new government that was more submissive to British interests. For Nasser, this was a most humiliating experience. The Free Officers plotted, and ten years later they changed the course of the region's history when they ousted the regime of King Farouk and Egypt's Wafd Party. The Egyptian monarchy was abolished soon after, and Nasser became the country's new leader.

Nasser's rise was troubling to Israeli leaders. He had fought them in the 1948 War, and he was the most capable of Arab leaders. His charisma, they feared, could enable him to unify Arabs across the region and become a real danger to Israel.

The 1948 War

What is usually labeled as the 1948 War actually had already begun in 1947. In the last chapter, we covered the United Nation's passing of the partition resolution in November 1947. The Arab Higher Committee (AHC) rejected it outright and called for protests and strikes. These, in turn, led to attacks on Jewish markets and shops in various cities. Mutual retaliations escalated very quickly into a complete civil war between Jews and Palestinians. On May 14, 1948, Jewish leaders

DOI: 10.4324/9781003536260-4

declared the State of Israel and therewith the civil war evolved into a war between the newly founded state and several Arab states.

The Civil War between Palestinians and the Yishuv

When the fighting began in December 1947, the Yishuv were in an advantageous position, both politically and militarily. Over the years and with British imperial help, the Jewish Agency had advanced into an efficient government. It demonstrated impressive economic strength and fundraising capabilities which allowed for the continuous purchase of European and American-made weaponry, complementing the Yishuv's own production. Through the civil war, the Haganah fielded about 35,000 troops, commanded by a central authority with an effective general staff. The paramilitary Irgun and the Lehi groups also contributed a few thousand fighters.[1]

Palestinians, on the other hand, because of significant British obstruction, continued to lack a functioning government. The AHC remained handicapped by factionalism and corruption. It proved unable to raise significant funds, and Palestinian production capacities were weak. Palestinians also lacked a national defense force. The main force was based on 400–500 village bands, each with anywhere between just a few to 100 members. There were also several independent Arab bands with up to 500 fighters. The Arab Liberation Army (ALA), comprised of over 5,000 mainly Syrian members, constituted the largest force. It had a few battalions, but each one operated independently. Finally, there were some groups of the Egyptian Muslim Brotherhood entering Palestine from the south.[2]

Despite the Yishuv's strength, Palestinians held the advantage of the initiative and were able to capture some strategic roads and besiege various Jewish settlements. By mid-December, however, the Yishuv's forces were engaging in successful counter attacks and soon they would dominate the conflict.[3] In April, the Haganah began with assaults on Jaffa and Haifa, two of the largest Palestinian cities, the Palestinian neighborhoods in West Jerusalem, as well as many other Palestinian towns and villages. It led to a mass exodus of Palestinians. Historians disagree as to whether the Jewish leadership had planned this to happen or whether it was a natural consequence of war.[4]

One fact here is that Israeli military forces made the return of fleeing Palestinians impossible by destroying hundreds of their villages and towns, which seems to indicate that a process of ethnic cleansing was indeed intended.[5] The most often-cited example of the intended terror on Palestinians and their flight is the Deir Yassin massacre. On April 9,

Irgun and Lehi forces invaded the village, embarking on an indiscriminate killing spree. When the assault concluded, about 100 Palestinians were dead, many of them women, children, and the elderly.[6] Although both the Jewish Agency and the Haganah condemned the massacre, it was also the case that the Yishuv very much benefited from the panic and the flight caused by these attacks.

Indeed, getting Palestinians to leave the land that was to become the State of Israel was exactly what Ben-Gurion and other Zionist leaders were aiming for.[7] In fact, the Zionist leadership had developed a plan, known as Plan Dalet, toward this end. Its content is summarized by the Israeli historian Ilan Pappe. It included "large-scale intimidation; laying siege and bombarding villages and population centres; setting fires to homes, properties and goods; expulsion; demolition; and, finally, planting mines among the rubble to prevent any of the expelled inhabitants from returning."[8]

By mid-May about 300,000 Palestinians had fled their homes in Palestine.[9] What for the Yishuv might have been a war of defense in December 1947 quickly evolved into a "war of conquest."[10] The Yishuv's forces secured not only the area assigned to them by the UN but also areas that had been assigned to Palestinians.

The First Arab-Israeli War

The British mandate over Palestine was to end on May 15. On the previous day, just a few hours before midnight, Jewish leaders gathered in the Tel Aviv Museum. Underneath a portrait of Theodor Herzl, David Ben-Gurion read the Declaration of Independence and then announced the establishment of the State of Israel. He was to be the country's first prime minister as well as its defense minister. In the United States, President Truman immediately recognized Israel diplomatically. The Soviet Union, as the world's second superpower, followed soon after.

Expectedly, the neighboring Arab states refused to recognize the newly proclaimed state and the civil war between the Yishuv and the Palestinians now became an inter-state war between Israel on the one side and Egypt, Jordan, Syria, Lebanon, Iraq, Saudi Arabia, and Yemen on the other. However, what appeared as a David versus Goliath situation was, in fact, not. Even though Israel's relatively small population was far outnumbered by the populations of the Arab countries, the balance of power on the battlefields was in favor of Israel. The Haganah, now renamed as the Israeli Defense Forces (IDF), marshaled about 35,000 soldiers. The Arab countries combined had only 25,000 soldiers.[11]

This power imbalance in Israel's favor continued as the war progressed. By July, the IDF had about 65,000 troops, while the Arab armies had about 40,000–50,000 soldiers in Palestine and the Egyptian Sinai. By December, the IDF marshalled nearly 100,000 troops.[12] The Arab countries did not match this increase, nor could they match the quality and quantity of Israeli weaponry, much of which was supplied by arms dealers in Europe and the U.S. Thus, although Israel was confronted by several Arab countries, it was, in fact, much more powerful than all of them put together, and the war played out accordingly.

Noteworthy here is also that individual Arab leaders were carried by ulterior motives. Most consequential were the machinations of Jordan's King Abdullah. Ambitioning for a greater Jordan that would include the Palestinian West Bank, he saw a Jewish state as a means toward that end. Jewish leaders, for their part, saw in Abdullah's motives an opportunity to have an acquiescing Arab leader as their neighbor, rather than a Palestinian state. This thus led to a secret understanding that Jordan and Israel would not attack each other; after the war, they would split the territory the UN had envisioned for a Palestinian state between them.[13] A few years later, the King paid the price for his schemes. In the summer of 1951 he was assassinated by a Palestinian gunman as he left Jerusalem's Haram al-Sharif after Friday prayers.

Thus, Jordan's military, which would have been Israel's strongest opponent, never crossed the border into Israel. Iraqi troops also did not cross the boundary to Israel, and Lebanese forces did not even cross into Palestinian territories. Aside from Syria's minor border crossings, the Egyptian army was more or less the only Arab force to advance deeper into Israel.[14] Largely on its own, however, it proved impotent to make any grounds against the much stronger and superior Israeli forces. By the time it came to a first UN truce on June 11, Israel was able to expand its territory further while simultaneously clearing dozens of Palestinian villages.

With the truce, the UN-appointed Swede Counte Folke Bernadotte formulated a settlement proposal: Palestine was to be "redivided."[15] The Jewish state would be in the UN-allotted area. It would now, however, exclude the Negev, but include the Galilee. Both states, furthermore, would be joined in a federal union. Jewish immigration would be decided by the UN, and Palestinian refugees would be able to return. To Israeli leaders the plan was a non-starter. They were winning the war, gaining additional territory and, therefore, not willing to consider such a compromise. Palestinians, for their part, could still not accept any imposed partition of their land.

On July 8, Egypt violated the truce, but now Israel emerged even stronger. It was able to boost its troop numbers much more than the

Arabs, and in the meantime had received valuable shipments of weapons.[16] A second truce began on July 18, but just before Bernadotte issued a new proposal, the Lehi assassinated the diplomat as he was sitting in his car. In mid-October, Israel violated the truce and was now determined to deliver the final blow to the enemy. In the north, Israeli forces seized all of the Galilee. In the center, Israel occupied large areas that were designated for the Palestinian state. In the south, Israel moved into the Negev Desert and advanced toward the Suez.

Leaders in the United States and Great Britain were troubled by both Israeli aggressiveness and disregard for the United Nations. Under pressure, negotiations toward armistices began in January, but the fighting continued into March.

The War's Aftermath

Before the war, Palestine numbered just shy of two million residents. Of these, about 1.3 million were Arabs and approximately 630,000 were Jews. Palestinians owned about 90 percent of the private lands, while the Yishuv owned only about 7 percent. After the war, Israel controlled 78 percent of the land. Well over 700,000 Palestinians, that is, more than half of the total Palestinian population, had fled and left their homes behind. This mass flight, so Israeli historian Benny Morris argues, was necessary for Israel to come into being:

> A Jewish State would not have come into being without the uprooting of 700,000 Palestinians. Therefore it was necessary to uproot them. There was no choice but to expel that population … [T]he need to establish this state in this place overcame the injustice that was done to the Palestinians by uprooting them.[17]

About 150,000 Palestinians remained within what was now Israel, subjugated to martial law until the mid-1960s.[18] What remained of Palestine came to be referred as the West Bank, controlled by Jordan, and the Gaza Strip, administered by Egypt. The dividing line between Israel and the West Bank became known as the Green Line, having been drawn on the map with a green pencil. The name Palestine was gone from the map.

In the months after the war, the warring parties signed armistices but not peace agreements. Arab leaders maintained their refusal to give legal recognition to Israel. For its part, Israel refused to withdraw from territory captured beyond the 1947 UN partition line, and it also refused to allow Palestinian refugees to return to their homes. On these two issues, the Arabs' argument was backed by international law; the forceful conquest of territory was impermissible and the UN declared in Resolution 194 that "refugees wishing to return to their homes should be permitted to do so at the earliest practicable date, and that compensation should be paid for the property of those choosing not to return and for loss of damage to property."

Israel, however, would not budge on the conquered territories. Its leaders insisted that they had neither a legal nor a moral obligation to allow Palestinian refugees to return. Because Arab states had started the war, they argued, it was their responsibility to absorb the Palestinian refugees into their own countries. Humiliated, these refugees were forced into the Gaza Strip, the many refugee camps across the West Bank, or the refugee camps of neighboring Arab countries. These camps were intended to be temporary, but they came to be lasting. Thousands of their homes were no more, as some 400 Palestinian villages and towns had been deliberately destroyed and new Jewish villages were now built on their ruins.[19] In 1950, Israel adopted the Law of Return. It permitted any Jew, born anywhere in the world and without any connection to Israel, to claim Israeli citizenship. Native Palestinian refugees and their descendants continue to remain barred from returning to their ancestral homeland.

As the years progressed, Palestinians crossed into what was now Israel, mostly to collect family property, harvest crops from the land they had worked on, or just to see relatives. However, some of these crossings were done by so-called *fedayeen* (resistance fighters) who targeted mainly Israeli facilities and infrastructure, but also people. Although they never really posed a serious military threat to Israel, they consistently led to disproportionate Israeli responses. An often-cited example occurred in the fall of 1953. Palestinian fighters had killed a mother and her two children. In return, the Israeli special forces raided the Palestinian West Bank village of Qibya, killing nearly seventy village residents and blowing up dozens of homes.[20] The raid was led by Ariel Sharon, a name that would accompany the Israeli-Palestinian conflict for decades to come.

The Suez War

After the 1948 War, the Israeli-Palestinian conflict began playing out increasingly in the contexts of regional politics as well as the global Cold War. One of the region's most significant figures at the time was Gamal Abdel Nasser whom we began this chapter with. After assuming the Egyptian presidency, Nasser quickly positioned himself as champion of a new pan-Arabism. He had fought Israel in the 1948 War but now was intent on exploring a lasting rapprochement. With the moderate foreign minister Moshe Sharett replacing Ben-Gurion as Israel's prime minister in mid-1954, there were indeed some hopes. However, these were quickly dashed by Defense Minister Pinhas Lavon and Military Chief of Staff Moshe Dayan who carried forth Ben-Gurion's legacy.

These hawkish Israeli leaders were bothered by Nasser's quest for economic and military aid from the U.S. and the implications such would have for the regional balance of power. Of further concern were British intentions to withdraw from the Sinai, where tens of thousands of British troops had been stationed since the 1948 War. This, Israelis feared, would expose the country's south to an Egyptian threat. A cunning plan was developed to counter these developments: Israeli agents, with Egyptian collaborators, were to plant bombs in Cairo's American and British facilities. The blame was to be put on an Islamic group. This, Israel calculated, would create anti-Egyptian sentiment in America and compel U.S. leaders to withdraw their support for Nasser. Furthermore, it would compel the British to maintain their troops in the Sinai.[21]

In July 1954, the agents moved to execute the plan, but they were caught and then either executed or jailed. Defense Minister Lavon was forced to resign from his post a few months later and David Ben-Gurion returned to government to take his place. In early 1955, there was an Israeli raid in Gaza where IDF companies, led again by Ariel Sharon, attacked Egyptian army bases in the land strip. Purportedly, the attack was in revenge for a fedayeen crossing sanctioned by Nasser. It resulted in the death of more than forty Egyptian and eight Israeli soldiers. For Nasser, the raid was a turning point. While he was initially intent on avoiding escalations with Israel, now his officers were training the fedayeen who were to make Israel bleed.[22]

Matters escalated yet further in September 1955 when Nasser ordered the Straits of Tiran to be closed, thereby preventing Israeli shipping to the harbor of Eilat in the Gulf of Aqaba. Intent on raising his standing in the Arab world, one month later Nasser had his military engage in joint exercises with Syrian forces. In Israel, Nasser's closing of the straits was considered a major provocation, and hawkish leaders like Moshe Dayan wanted war with Egypt rather sooner than later in order to capitalize on Israel's tremendous power advantage at the time. When Ben-Gurion assumed the premiership for a second time in November, the possibility of war indeed became more likely.

As we saw a few paragraphs earlier, this was also the time when Middle Eastern politics came to be more entangled with world politics and the Cold War. When, in the summer of 1955, an American-Egyptian arms deal fell through, Nasser turned to the Soviet Union. Needless to say, his move contributed to increasing irritations in the U.S. Nevertheless, in December 1955, Washington offered funds for the building of the Aswan Dam on the Nile River, a project of crucial importance for the expansion of Egypt's farmland, production of electricity and, therewith, the modernization of Egypt. However, when Nasser recognized Communist China in May 1956, he had finally gone too far. Washington withdrew its financial offer, a step that would have far-reaching consequences.

On July 25, Nasser took the extraordinary step of nationalizing the Suez Canal so as to create substantial revenue from passing ships for the planned dam. The canal, of course, had been an imperialist project. For Britain, it remained a gateway to Asia as well as to its oil interests in the Persian Gulf. France was also affected as it was a principal shareholder of the canal. Moreover, Nasser had been an irritation to both British and French leaders for a while. The British were maddened by Nasser's support for nationalist challenges to Britain's influence in Iraq, the Gulf, and other parts of the Arab world. French leaders, for their part, were more than irritated that Nasser had been supporting rebels against the French in France's North African colonies. With Nasser's nationalization act, the time had come to get rid of him.

Nasser's actions were legal under international law, however, and so the British and the French needed a pretense for his removal. Thus, Israel was introduced into the scheming. In late October 1956, leaders of the three countries convened at the outskirts of Paris to discuss their plan. It is a bit confusing, but here are its central aspects: Israel was to invade the Sinai and head toward the Suez. The British and the French were to call for a truce, demanding an Egyptian and Israeli withdrawal 10 miles from the canal. As Israeli forces would, in fact, not have advanced within such a proximity of the canal yet, this demand really meant that the IDF would be able to continue advancing toward the canal. Egyptian forces, on the other hand, would have to retreat from their positions. According to the trio's calculations, Nasser would not accept, making it easy for the group to blame him for ongoing hostilities, which would ultimately justify British and French military intervention. They would retake the canal while Nasser would lose face and be forced to give up his presidency.[23]

On October 29, the trio began its assault and, at first, it played out as intended. As Nasser rejected the ultimatum, British and French forces bombed the Egyptian air force and their paratroopers occupied the Suez Canal zone. The IDF, in the meantime, was advancing far into the Sinai. The plan was suddenly disrupted, however, when both U.S. and Soviet leaders became deeply concerned that the Suez conflict could drag them into a confrontation. They moved quickly to push through a UN resolution demanding an immediate withdrawal.

The War's Aftermath

Despite the forced withdrawal of its forces, Israel scored a victory. Most importantly, it achieved the reopening of the Gulf of Aqaba. Moreover, fedayeen bases in Gaza were destroyed, and United Nations Emergency Forces (UNEF) were now assigned to the Sharm al-Shaykh area to provide security. For Great Britain and France, however, the war was a total blunder. Their standing in the Middle East had already been in stark decline, but the Suez episode made clear that their days were numbered. The U.S. had already begun the process of taking their place and henceforth it would be the predominant patron in the region.

On the Egyptian side, Nasser would have been about to face a humiliating military defeat were it not for the superpowers' intervention. Instead, it became to a tremendous political victory. By nationalizing the Suez Canal, in the perception of Arabs across the region, he had stood up to Israel and to British and French imperialism. In 1958, he realized an initial step of his long-standing pan-Arabist dream. Egypt unified with Syria, and he was now the president of the United Arab Republic. It was a short-lived position, however, as the union dissolved in 1961.

The 1967 War

In January 1961, John F. Kennedy became the new American president. His administration considered Arab nationalism to be a barrier against communism, thereby serving America's prime concern in the Middle East. Palestinians also put some hope in Kennedy as he had promised to support a UN Conciliation Commission toward seeking a resolution to the Palestinian refugee issue. These ambitions faltered quickly, however, as Israel rejected the return of more than a symbolic number of refugees. In November 1963, Kennedy was assassinated and was succeeded by Lyndon Johnson. Johnson was a strong supporter of Zionism and, already in his first year in office, the new American president provided Israel with the most advanced weapons the U.S. had.[24]

The next showdown between Israelis and Arabs was brewing in the meantime. Tensions rose over Israel's water diversions from the Jordan River, reducing the supplies for Arab countries. At its January 1964 Cairo meeting, in addition to discussing the danger of Israel, the Arab League created a Palestinian parliament, namely the Palestine National Council (PNC), as well as the Palestine Liberation Organization (PLO). The Council's Charter judged the 1947 UN partition resolution to be illegal and defined Zionism as "a colonialist movement, aggressive and expansionist in its goals, racist in its configuration, and fascist in its means and aims ..."[25] The elimination of Israel and the creation of a Palestinian state were the ultimate goal.

Egypt, in the meantime, with the help of Soviet military aid, was growing stronger, and so was Syria. Encouraged by Moscow, the two countries agreed to a mutual defense alliance in 1966. Israel was not deterred, however. It engaged in provocative maneuvers in the demilitarized zone along the Syrian border with the goal of gradually capturing more land. An initial shooting fight soon escalated into aerial dogfights, with the Israeli air force proving dominant as it downed six Syrian planes and reached far inland toward the capital city of Damascus. The countdown to another Arab-Israeli war had begun.

The ultimate escalation began on May 13, 1967, when Moscow informed Cairo and Damascus of Israeli troop movements near the Syrian border. It was a false alarm. Not knowing this, however, Nasser declared a state of emergency and ordered UNEF to withdraw from the Sinai. They were to be replaced by Egyptian troops, and the Egyptian–Israeli border thus became a military fault line. After Israel called upon its reserves on May 19, Nasser announced that Egyptian forces were closing the Strait of Tiran to Israeli shipping. He had done this more than a decade prior and gotten away with it. This time around, his brinkmanship would come to cost him a high price.

Israeli leaders cited this move as a justification for war, considering it a vital threat to their economy. More importantly, however, it was an opportune occasion to put Nasser in his place. It was also an opportune moment to lay claim on the long-desired West Bank and to illustrate the power and sophistication of the IDF. It had about 250,000 well-skilled troops. It also had 1,100 tanks and 400 artillery pieces and heavy mortars. Its air force held just shy of 200 superior fighter jets, with plentiful pilots who were supported by a sophisticated command system and highly capable ground crews.[26]

The Arab militaries, by contrast, were not nearly as well equipped. Their training was deficient, as was their leadership. The Egyptian forces featured between 150,000 and 180,000 troops, as well as around 900 tanks and 800 artillery pieces. The air force held about 230 fighter aircraft, many poorly maintained, and notably fewer trained pilots than aircraft. Jordanian forces consisted of 56,000 troops with nearly 290 tanks and 160 artillery pieces and heavy mortars. Its air force held two dozen fighter jets. Finally, the Syrian army fielded 70,000 troops with about 300 tanks as well as 265 artillery pieces and heavy mortars. It also had 92 fighter jets.[27]

Although the combined numbers of Arab militaries were formidable, the fact was that the IDF had a qualitative superiority in almost every sphere. In the U.S., the expectation was that Israel would dominate in any conflict against Arab enemies. As one official put it, "The intelligence was absolutely flat on the fact that the Israelis ... could mop up the Arabs in no time at all."[28]

In the early morning hours of June 5, Israel displayed its overwhelming power with a surprise attack on Egyptian airfields, destroying about 200 aircraft. Soon afterwards, the air forces of Syria and Jordan faced the same fate. The Israeli army overwhelmed the Arab forces and moved into Gaza, East Jerusalem, the West Bank, Egypt's Sinai, and Syria's Golan Heights. Israel won one of the most decisive victories that the modern world has seen. Egypt suffered the most casualties, with up to 15,000 dead; Jordan lost about 800, and Syria about 500. Israel recorded about 800 casualties.[29]

Although the crucial fighting really lasted only two or three days, the conflict is often referred to as the "Six Day War," especially by people sympathetic to Israel. The phrasing is meant to invoke a biblical connotation, making the victory appear to be God-given. Of special meaning was the capture of East Jerusalem, the ancient capital of David and Solomon's kingdom, but now inhabited mainly by Palestinians. At the end of the month, Prime Minister Levy Eshkol declared that henceforth all of Jerusalem would be Israel's eternal capital. The UN General Assembly condemned the annexation. But this didn't matter to the Eshkol government, which was intent on cleansing the conquered areas from as many Palestinians as possible. It started in the Moroccan quarters, where the homes of hundreds of residents were destroyed along with two mosques from the 12th century.[30]

Much like the 1948 War, the 1967 War led to a mass flight. About 200,000 Palestinians became refugees. Palestinians described the experience as a *Naksa*, a setback. An independent Palestine would remain the goal, but it would become increasingly elusive.

The War's Aftermath

With the 1967 War, Israel emerged as a regional superpower in the Middle East, one equipped with the capability of nuclear weapons. It suited Washington leaders' strategic interests. They had long been eager to recruit reliable allies toward safeguarding American political and economic interests in the Middle East. This was the time when the much-mentioned special relationship between the U.S. and Israel really took off. The U.S. would come to acquiesce in Israel's lasting occupation of Palestinian lands and made certain that it would always maintain a military advantage over any possible coalition of its Arab neighbors. Over time, Israel would prove itself of value to U.S. interest and meddling not only in the Middle East but also in other parts of the world.

Arab leaders, for their part, met in Sudan's capital Khartoum at the end of August and declared their famous "three nos" – no peace with Israel, no recognition of Israel, and no negotiation with Israel. This sounded strong, but in fact the three noes were preceded by an emphasis on international diplomacy toward Israeli withdrawal from conquered territories in the June War. But even here, Arab leaders possessed no leverage. This showed, for example, in UN debates about a post-war resolution. Arabs argued for language stating that Israel must withdraw from *all* the territories occupied in the war. Leaders in Israel and the U.S., however, objected to any such wording, and it was they who got their way.

On November 22, the UN Security Council issued Resolution 242, which would become a continuous reference for settlement efforts in the years and decades ahead. It emphasized the "inadmissibility of the acquisition of territory by war" and called for the "withdrawal of Israeli armed forces from territories occupied in the recent conflict," the "termination of all claims or states of belligerency and respect for and acknowledgement of the sovereignty, territorial integrity, and political independence of every State in the area," the guarantee of "freedom of navigation through international waterways in the area," and a "just settlement of the refugee problem."[31]

Expectedly, Israel used the omitted definitive article "the" before "territories occupied in the recent conflict" in the resolution to argue that while it was required to withdraw from *some* territories, it was not required to withdraw from *all* territories and also not from any territory in its entirety. It withdrew from the Egyptian Sinai, but it remained in the Syrian Golan Heights, the Palestinian Gaza Strip, East Jerusalem, and the West Bank. In the West Bank, it expanded its settlements, justifying this by reference to divine rights and security needs. Israel was now an occupying power, ruling forcefully over nearly 1.5 million Palestinians.

Conclusion

In 1947, the UN partition plan allotted 55 percent of Mandatory Palestine to Israel. With the 1948 War, Israel seized another 23 percent and was now in control of 78 percent of the land. For Jews, this was a war of independence; they gained statehood on a territory much larger than intended. Palestinians refer to the war as al-Nakba – a catastrophe had befallen them. Many hundreds of thousands became refugees. As history would show, the 1948 War was only the beginning of forthcoming wars and annexations with consequences for Palestinians and Israelis, alongside ramifications for regional stability and peace as well as for world politics. The 1956 Suez War drew in international powers and contributed to Cold War tensions, as did the 1967 War. Palestinians, for their part, lost all their lands.

Israel was strong and did what it had the power to do. Palestinians resisted, but it was to no avail. This leads us, once again, to ponder some aspects of justice. Given the fundamental fact that Palestinians lost more and more of their land and homes, and given power realities between Israel and Palestine, the question is sometimes asked whether Palestinians should have accepted partition in 1947. By attempting to fight it, they came to lose everything and found themselves perpetually humiliated. On one level, this seems to be a simple question of pragmatism. To Palestinians, however, it was unfathomable. It was their land and nobody had the right to partition it. To them, the international community and the UN failed to do what was just and right.

Suggested Further Readings

Kaplan, Amy. 2018. *Our American Israel: The Story of an Entangled Alliance*. Cambridge, MA: Harvard University Press.

Masalah, Nur. 2012. *The Palestine Nakba: Decolonising History, Narrating the Subaltern, Reclaiming Memory*. London: Zed Books.

Morris, Benny. 1993. *Israel's Border Wars, 1949–1956*. New York: Oxford University Press.

Morris, Benny. 2004. *The Birth of the Palestinian Refugee Problem Revisited*. New York: Cambridge University Press.

Morris, Benny. 2009. *1948: The First Arab-Israeli War*. New Haven, CT: Yale University Press.

Pappe, Ilan. 2006. *The Ethnic Cleansing of Palestine*. Oxford: Oneworld Publications.

Rogan, Eugene and Avi Shlaim, eds. 2001. *The War for Palestine: Rewriting the History of 1948*. Cambridge: Cambridge University Press.

Sayegh, Fayez. 2017. *The Palestinian Refugees*. London: Forgotten Books.

Segev, Tom. 2007. *1967: Israel, the War, and the Year that Transformed the Middle East*. New York: Metropolitan Books.

Segev, Tom. 2018. *1949: The First Israelis*. New York: Free Press.

Notes

1 Benny Morris. 2009. *1948: The First Arab-Israeli War*. New Haven, CT: Yale University Press, p. 86; Charles Smith. 2004. *Palestine and the Arab-Israeli Conflict*, 5th edition. New York: Bedford/St. Martin's, p. 191.
2 Benny Morris, *1948: The First Arab-Israeli War*, pp. 82–85; Benny Morris. 1999. *Righteous Victims*. New York: Alfred Knopf, pp. 194–196.
3 Benny Morris, *Righteous Victims*, pp. 196–197; Khaled Elgindy. 2019. *Blind Spot: America and the Palestinians, from Balfour to Trump*. Washington, DC: Brookings Institution Press, p. 39.
4 Benny Morris. 1988. *The Birth of the Palestinian Refugee Problem, 1947–1949*. Cambridge: Cambridge University Press, p. 286.
5 Ian Black. 2017. *Enemies and Neighbors: Arabs and Jews in Palestine and Israel, 1917–2017*. New York: Atlantic Monthly Press, p. 115; David Lesch. 2008. *The Arab-Israeli Conflict*. New York: Oxford University Press, p. 137; Nur Masallah. 1992. *Expulsion of the Palestinians*. Washington, DC: Institute for Palestine Studies; Ilan Pappe. 2006. *The Ethnic Cleansing of Palestine*. Oxford: Oneworld Publications; Rosemarie Esber. 2009. *Under the Cover of War*. Alexandria, VA: Arabicus Books; Avi Shlaim. 2014. *The Iron Wall*. New York: W.W. Norton, pp. 36–37; Simha Flapan. 1987. *The Birth of Israel*. New York: Pantheon Books, p. 42; Uri Avnery. 2008. *Israel's Vicious Cycle*, edited by Sara Powell. London: Pluto Press, p. 13.
6 Rashid Khalidi. 2006. *The Iron Cage*. Boston, MA: Beacon Press, p. 133.
7 Daniel Gordis. 2016. *Israel: A Concise History of a Nation Reborn*. New York: HarperCollins Publishers, p. 160; Simha Flapan, *The Birth of Israel*, p. 84; Noura Erakat. 2019. *Justice for Some*. Stanford, CA: Stanford University Press, p. 48.
8 Ilan Pappe, *The Ethnic Cleansing of Palestine*, p. xii.
9 Gudrun Kraemer. 2008. *A History of Palestine*. Princeton, NJ: Princeton University Press, p. 315; Charles Smith, *Palestine and the Arab-Israeli Conflict*, p. 194; Simha Flapan, *The Birth of Israel*, p. 89.
10 Benny Morris, *The First Arab-Israeli War*, p. 119.
11 David Lesch, *The Arab-Israeli Conflict*, p. 139; James Gelvin. 2014. *The Israel-Palestine Conflict*. Cambridge: Cambridge University Press, pp. 131–132; Neil Caplan. 2010. *The Israel-Palestine Conflict: Contested Histories*. Chichester: Wiley-Blackwell, pp. 112–113; Charles Smith, *Palestine and the Arab-Israeli Conflict*, p. 196; Avi Shlaim. 1995. "The Debate About 1948." *International Journal of Middle East Studies* 27: 287–304 (referenced here, p. 295).
12 Benny Morris, *Righteous Victims*, p. 217; Gudrun Krämer, *A History of Palestine*, pp. 315–316.
13 Simha Flapan, *The Birth of Israel*, p. 8; Benny Morris, *Righteous Victims*, p. 221.
14 Rashid Khalidi, *The Iron Cage*, p. xxxix.
15 Benny Morris, *Righteous Victims*, p. 237.
16 Benny Morris, *Righteous Victims*, pp. 235–236.
17 Quoted in Ari Shavit. 2004. *Survival of the Fittest*. Haaretz (January 8).
18 Rashid Khalidi. *The Iron Cage*, p. 1; Ilan Pappe. 2017. *Ten Myths About Israel*. New York: Verso, p. 48.
19 Uri Avnery, *Israel's Vicious Cycle*, pp. 13–14; Khaled Elgindy, *Blind Spot*, p. 48; Ran Greenstein. 2020. "Israel, Palestine, and Apartheid." *Insight Turkey* 22: 73–92.

20 David Lesch, *The Arab-Israel Conflict*, p. 170; Charles Smith, *Palestine and the Arab-Israeli Conflict*, p. 224.
21 Benny Morris, *Righteous Victims*, p. 282; Avi Shlaim, *The Iron Wall*, p. 118.
22 David Lesch, *The Arab-Israeli Conflict*, p. 176; James Gelvin, *The Israel-Palestine Conflict*, p. 173; Avi Shlaim, *The Iron Wall*, p. 136.
23 David Lesch, *The Arab-Israeli Conflict*, pp. 179–183.
24 Georhe Lenczowski. 1990. *American Presidents and the Middle East*. Durham, NC: Duke University Press, pp. 115.
25 Benny Morris, *1948: The First Arab-Israeli War*, p. 110; Avi Shlaim, *The Iron Wall*, p. 245; Khaled Elgindy, *Blind Spot*, p. 64.
26 Benny Morris, *Righteous Victims*, pp. 311–313.
27 Benny Morris, *Righteous Victims*, pp. 311–313.
28 Sandy Tolan. 2011. *June 7: The Anniversary Nobody Remembers*. Al Jazeera (June 7). Available at www.aljazeera.com/opinions/2011/6/7/june-7-the-anniversary-nobody-remembers
29 Benny Morris, *Righteous Victims*, p. 327.
30 Ian Black, *Enemies and Neighbors*, p. 182.
31 The resolution can be seen at https://digitallibrary.un.org/record/90717?ln=en&v=pdf

5 Toward Permanent Occupation

Although Yasir Arafat was not born in Palestine, he was one of its most ardent defenders. Born in Egypt's capital Cairo in August 1929 to a father from Gaza and a mother from Jerusalem, his first experiences in Palestine occurred in the mid-1930s. His mother had died, and the young Yasir had been sent to live with an uncle in Jerusalem. It was the time of the Arab Revolt, but being so young, the ensuing events very likely didn't register much with him. His interest in the Palestinian national cause came soon though, and in the 1948 War, he was engaged in both the acquisition of weapons for Arab fighters and in some small-scale operations.

After the war, Arafat enrolled as a civil engineering student at Cairo's King Fuad University where he also took over as leader of the Palestinian Student Union. Upon his graduation in 1956, he went to Kuwait to work as a civil engineer. His passion remained with the Palestinian cause, however, and so it was that in 1959, together with a small group of like-minded others, he founded the Palestine Liberation Movement. The name for the movement in Arabic is *Harakat al-Tahrir al-Filiastinya*. The reversed acronym spells *Fatah* (conquest), and this is the name by which the movement came to be known. Arafat, with his trademark black and white checkered *keffiyeh* (head cloth), would stand at the helm of Palestinian resistance for nearly four decades.

The Expansion of Israel

We ended the preceding chapter with the 1967 War. Israel occupied all of Palestine now and started building military posts, such as those in the Jordan Valley, and settlements in East Jerusalem and the West Bank. These were a fundamental violation of the 1949 Fourth Geneva Convention, which constitutes a foundation of humanitarian international law. According to the Convention, "The occupying power shall not

DOI: 10.4324/9781003536260-5

deport or transfer parts of its own civilian population into the territories it occupies." There is a simple reason for this prohibition, namely to ensure that the occupation is temporary and to inhibit the occupying power from establishing long-term interests in the occupied land which would stand in the way of a solution. The UN has condemned these settlement projects many times over the years, yet they continue to this day.

Israeli leaders chose to contravene international law. It was Arab aggression that forced the situation, they argued. The territories were not occupied but "disputed" and, as such, they were not prohibited by the Geneva Convention. To be sure, there were also voices, including Prime Minister Levi Eshkol's, that pointed to problems that the continued occupation and the settlements would come to pose in the future. The most crucial one was that with its expansion, Israel would have jurisdiction over a growing number of Palestinians, without giving them equal political and civil rights, however. Over time, so the warning went, Israel would evolve into an apartheid state. Such cautionary voices remained unheeded. We will cover the term apartheid more in Chapter 6. Here it suffices to say that it describes the domination of one racial or ethnic group by another one.

The War of Attrition

Amid the Israeli expansion, the Israeli-Palestinian conflict continued to play out against the backdrop of regional politics and the Cold War. In Cairo, the 1967 defeat was weighing heavily on President Nasser. He lamented the Palestinian situation, but what bothered him most was the loss of the Egyptian Sinai. He could not afford another full-scale war to regain it, so he started what came to be referred to as the War of Attrition in the spring of 1969. Through artillery fights across the Suez Canal as well as aerial provocations, Nasser hoped to wear Israel down and compel its withdrawal. At the very least, however, he hoped for an international intervention to end the occupation.

Just a few weeks earlier, Richard Nixon had succeeded Lyndon Johnson in the White House. One of the new administration's chief aims was to ease Cold War tensions. Toward that end, there would need to be stability between the superpower allies, and thus the war of attrition was indeed a concern for Washington. In December, Secretary of State William Rogers proposed what came to be known as the Rogers Plan. Based on UN Resolution 242, it set forth an Israeli withdrawal to the pre-1967 borders, as well as a return of Palestinian refugees or the payment of compensation. The Israeli government, now led by Golda Meir, rejected the plan out of hand.

Israel also wouldn't allow itself to be worn down as Nasser had hoped. Quite the opposite. Its fighter jets penetrated deeply into Egypt, and Nasser was on the verge of another humiliating defeat. When Moscow stepped in and provided Egypt with military aid, pilots, and mechanics, it complicated the strategic situation between the superpowers. Washington leaders worried that Israel might down a Soviet pilot or otherwise provoke a superpower confrontation, so they pressured Israel toward negotiations in August 1970.[1]

Palestinian Isolation

Palestinians, in the meantime, were learning that they could not rely on Arab leaders and that they had to fend for themselves. Fatah quickly grew to be the biggest faction in the Palestine Liberation Organization (PLO), and in 1969, Arafat became its chairman. The PLO was an umbrella organization to diverse factions and a major rival to Fatah was the Popular Front for the Liberation of Palestine (PFLP), led by George Habash, a refugee and physician from Lydda. Yet another faction in the PLO was the Democratic Front for the Liberation of Palestine (DFLP) under the leadership of Nayif Hawatamah. All of these groups shared in common that they were secular.

One of the PLO's first initiatives was to advocate for what was Mandatory Palestine some decades earlier to become a single democratic state for all its citizen, Jews and Palestinians alike. To Israeli leaders such a suggestion seemed not only ridiculous, coming from a group they regarded as terrorists, but it was also anathema to their Zionist ambitions for a Jewish state. Absent any political prospects, the PLO was compelled to continue its guerilla campaigns. After the West Bank had been occupied in the 1967 War, the organization had transferred its bases to Jordan and came to marshal thousands of fighters. The Kingdom became the battleground for the PLO and Israeli forces, thereby also worsening the friction between the PLO and King Hussein, who was seen by Palestinians as a Western puppet.[2]

Matters came to a spectacular head on September 6, 1970. In an effort to draw the world's attention to the Palestinian plight and force the release of Palestinian prisoners, the PFLP hijacked several international airliners. Three of them were directed to an old airbase just outside the Jordanian capital Amman (another one was flown to Cairo). After some days of intense negotiations, the crews and passengers were released, but the planes were blown up. Hussein ordered his troops to eliminate the PLO from Jordan. In a ten-day confrontation that came to be known as Black September, the Palestinian guerillas were no match for the heavily equipped Jordanian army. The fighting left about 5,000 people dead and the PLO fled to Lebanon.[3]

The 1973 War

As Black September was unfolding in Jordan, in Egypt President Nasser died from a heart attack on September 28. He was succeeded by Vice President Anwar Sadat who, like Nasser, came from the ranks of the Free Officers. He knew well that his standing would depend on his ability to reclaim the Sinai. A ceasefire in the War of Attrition had just been brokered and the Swedish UN envoy Gunnar Jarring was working on a peace plan. Like the earlier Rogers Plan, it was based on UN Resolution 242. Expectedly, as it had rejected the Rogers Plan, the Israeli government also rejected the Jarring Plan. What Israeli leaders wanted were negotiations without any prior conditions that would curtail their Greater Israel ambitions, such as Resolution 242 did.

Sadat felt increasingly compelled toward a war, and in Syria's president Hafiz al-Assad, he had a willing partner. In the 1967 War, al-Assad had been Syria's defense minister, and since the loss of the Golan Heights, he felt a personal responsibility to reclaim the territory. Together, they marshalled over one and a half million troops, 4,500 tanks, 3,400 artillery pieces, and 1,080 aircraft. Israel had somewhat over 100,000 standing troops and about 300,000 reserves, 2,200 tanks, about 1,000 artillery pieces, and 550 fighter planes. It thus seemed that the Arabs had a significant power advantage this time around. In a more nuanced comparison, however, Israel was far ahead of its Arab foes. In good part, this was due to its vast technological superiority. Moreover, although Moscow supplied the Arab forces with tanks and guns as well as MiG-21 aircraft, Washington provided Israel with more of pretty much everything.[4]

Sadat and al-Assad were well aware of the Israeli military superiority, but they calculated that a surprise attack would create an advantage. The selected date was October 6, Yom Kippur for Jews, and the tenth day of the holy month of Ramadan for Muslims. Religion, however, did not have much to do with the selection of this date. Rather, it was because this day would be preceded by a night of ideal moonlight and water currents and tide conditions that would be tactically beneficial for crossing the Suez Canal onto the Sinai. Thus, on the selected date, Egyptian forces established bridges across the canal and stormed over with five infantry divisions and massive artillery. In the northern Golan Heights, Syrian forces launched tank offensives. At times, it seemed as if Syrian forces could venture into the Galilee and reach Israel's heartland.[5]

Israel was in shock, but just as things were going well for the Arab duo, their fortunes turned as a result of a betrayal. Sadat and al-Assad's common goal was to regain the territories they lost in 1967. Toward this end, they pursued very different strategies, however. While al-Assad aimed at forcing the recapture militarily, Sadat's goal was to engage only in a limited military campaign and then proceed diplomatically. His intention was to reclaim just enough land east of the Suez Canal. Demonstrating Israeli vulnerability, he hoped for negotiations involving the U.S. Thus, soon after Egyptian troops crossed the Canal, they were ordered to stop.[6]

Sadat had left al-Assad in the dark about his plans, and his calculations proved terribly wrong. The Egyptian forces' defensive posture after the crossing allowed Israel to mobilize its reserves, and the initial Arab strategic advantage gave way to Israel's superior power. Within days, the IDF was able to turn the tables as it defeated Egyptian columns and retook not only much of the Sinai but also advanced to the west of the Suez. On the northern front, after Syrian forces had failed to march further, the IDF recaptured the Golan Heights and ventured within 30 miles of the Syrian capital Damascus.

U.S. military aid was instrumental for Israel's victory, but it would lead to a backlash of another kind. The Organization of Petroleum Exporting Countries (OPEC) had been founded in 1960. It had twelve members, nine of which were Muslim-majority countries. Saudi Arabia's King Faysal initiated a collective oil embargo toward those countries that supported Israel, foremost the U.S., of course. It led to a serious economic crisis, pressing Washington to work in tandem with Moscow to pass UN Resolution 338 on October 22. It called for an immediate ceasefire, a withdrawal to pre-war lines, and a resumption of negotiations based on UN Resolution 242 from 1967. Hostilities stopped on October 25.

The War's Aftermath

The War left anywhere between 8,000 and 22,000 Egyptians and Syrians dead. Israeli casualties were numbered close to 3,000.[7] The Jewish state had been seriously injured. Many Israelis felt that the country came to the brink of a disaster and held the Labor Party leadership accountable. Within a few months, Prime Minister Golda Meier left the government and was succeeded by Yitzhak Rabin, while Defense Minister Moshe Dayan was replaced by Shimon Peres.

Sadat, on the other hand, felt victorious, despite the fact that he was saved only by a UN resolution. The superpowers' intervention provided him with the opportunity for negotiations, his pre-war goal. The political settlement was to be mediated by U.S. Secretary of State Henry Kissinger, who embarked on his famous shuttle diplomacy between the

Israeli and Arab capitals. By January 1974, after many trips back and forth, he brokered the Sinai I agreement between Israel and Egypt. Israel was to withdraw from the west bank of the Suez Canal and some 20 miles inland from the east bank. Egypt, committed to a substantial force reduction in the Sinai, and a UN-monitored buffer zone was established between the two armies. One year later, Sinai II took the military disengagement and political settlement further.

Hafiz al-Assad, not surprisingly, felt betrayed by Sadat and humiliated by Israel. When meeting with Kissinger, he tended to pose as a tough negotiator. In reality, however, he did not achieve much. Israel retained large parts of the Golan Heights and henceforth UN Disengagement Observer Forces (UNDOF) would serve as a buffer between Israeli and Syrian forces.

From Armed Resistance to Diplomacy

Although Sadat, al-Assad, and other Arab leaders often presented themselves as advocates for the Palestinian people, they were, in fact, pursuing nothing more than their own national interests. Palestinians, once again, were left in the lurch. Israel was not going to withdraw from their lands unless it would somehow be forced to. Thus, various Palestinian groups became more committed to acts of armed resistance.

The hijacking of airplanes was a repeated strategy as it generated much international media coverage. Perhaps the most notorious incident, however, occurred at the 1972 Munich Olympic Games. It was done by the Black September group, which had named itself after the PLO's traumatic experience in Jordan a few years earlier. On September 5, eight gunman invaded Israeli athletes' apartments in the Olympic village. Two Israelis were shot dead as they tried to flee and nine were taken as hostages. The group demanded the release of 200 imprisoned Palestinians. Israel rejected the demands, and as German special forces launched a rescue operation, all of the hostages were killed.

Such acts did not lead to any progress for the Palestinian people. Instead, their national cause came to be equated with terrorism and it soon compelled the PLO to reevaluate its strategies. It denounced Black September, and while it did not totally repudiate armed struggle, it put a much stronger emphasis on political strategies. Moreover, at the twelfth meeting of the Palestinian National Council held in June 1974 in Cairo, the PLO abstained from insisting that a Palestinian state had to be established across all of historic Palestine; this was the PLO's first public acknowledgement that Israel was here to stay and that it was open to some compromise. It was also an acknowledgement of the overwhelming power disparities between itself and Israel.

The PLO's new course seemed promising. Already in September 1973 had the Non-Aligned Movement (NAM) invited the PLO to join the organization as an observer and so did the Organization of African Unity. In October 1974, the Arab League decided that the PLO should be the "sole legitimate representative of the Palestinian people." One month later, Arafat spoke at the UN. With the U.S. and Israeli ambassadors out, Arafat began his speech by committing the PLO to NAM's goal to end imperialism and to achieve self-determination for all nations. He bemoaned the Palestinian struggle against colonialism and the removal of Palestine's native people. Palestine, he said, should be a democratic home to all faiths. He concluded with his famous words, "I come bearing an olive branch and a freedom fighter's gun. Do not let the olive branch fall from my hand."

Arafat's speech was received with a standing ovation, and shortly afterwards, the UN passed two resolutions. One of them assigned the PLO an observer status at the UN. The other one attributed to the Palestinian people "inalienable rights," including "the right to self-determination without external interference" and "the right to national independence and sovereignty."[8] Subsequently, some European governments authorized the opening of PLO offices in their capitals. In January 1976, a resolution was drafted for the Security Council. Supported by various Arab states and the Soviet Union, it called for Israel's withdrawal to the 1967 borders, a two-state solution, and a right of refugees to return to their homes. Israel, however, refused to consider the proposal and the U. S. issued its veto, thereby terminating the resolution.

By the second half of the 1970s, the PLO's standing seemed to be very different than it was at the beginning of the decade. It had revived the Palestinian national cause and had attained increased attention on the world stage. When it came to the U.S., however, it proved unable to obtain any recognition. Moreover, progress for the Palestinian people in their daily lives remained absent.

The Rise of Likud

After the 1973 War, the Israeli people held the leadership of the Labor Party responsible not only for the near-disaster of the war but also for mounting domestic challenges. The right-oriented Likud alliance gradually rose in popularity and ultimately won the 1977 elections. Its victory didn't bode well for any progress in the Israeli-Palestinian conflict. It stood in the tradition of Ze'ev Jabotinsky whom we encountered in Chapter 3 and who, already in the 1920s, had insisted on a Greater Israel. Accordingly, Likud's election manifesto stated:

> The right of the Jewish people to the Land of Israel is eternal, and is an integral part of its right to security and peace. Judea and Samaria [the occupied West Bank] shall therefore not be relinquished …; between the sea and the Jordan, there will be Jewish sovereignty alone.[9]

Menachem Begin became prime minister. Having lost various family members in the Holocaust, he believed Arabs could prove just as dangerous to the Jewish people as had Germans some decades earlier. In the 1940s, Begin had led the Irgun terrorist group with the goal of realizing a Greater Israel. He failed then, but now he saw another opportunity. Thus, in the years to come, the confiscation of ever more Palestinian land accelerated, as did the building of new settlements. These were supported not only by politicians but also by various settler movements, the most prominent of which was the militant-religious *Gush Emunim* (the Bloc of the Faithful), a group for which the settlements in the West Bank were a God-given obligation.

The Camp David Accords

In August 1974, a politically disgraced Richard Nixon was forced to resign. He was succeeded by Vice-President Gerald Ford. In 1976, however, when running for a full term, Ford was defeated by Jimmy Carter, who assumed the American presidency in January 1977. Arab-Israeli peace figured prominently on his administration's foreign policy agenda, as it was seen to constitute the core of the problems in the Middle East. Regarding the Palestinian situation specifically, he was aiming for an Israeli withdrawal to the 1967 lines. Under pressure from the Israeli government, the administration soon abandoned its push for the inclusion of Palestinians in the Arab-Israeli peace negotiations.[10]

It was thus only on the Egyptian-Israeli front where progress would occur. In November 1977, Anwar Sadat announced to Egyptian parliamentarians that he was willing to go anywhere for the sake of peace, including the Israeli Knesset. Later that month he indeed arrived at Tel Aviv's Ben-Gurion Airport, the first official visit to Israel by an Arab leader, and, moreover, the most powerful Arab leader. Addressing the Knesset, Sadat accepted Israel's legitimacy and insisted that it should enjoy safety among her Arab neighbors. He also spoke on behalf of the Palestinians, warning that the peace would remain volatile unless Palestinians were included. Begin, for his part, talked about a host of grievances against Arabs. He rejected going beyond Israel's established positions and he ignored the Palestinian issue completely.

To move the Arab-Israeli rapprochement forward, President Carter invited both leaders to the presidential retreat Camp David in Maryland. When the talks began on September 5, they quickly proved very challenging. As had become evident already in Jerusalem, Sadat and Begin didn't have much sympathy for each other. At times they shouted at each other and even refused to be in the same room, forcing Carter to shuttle back and forth between their cabins. Despite such difficulties, on September 17, the talks concluded with the Camp David Accords, featuring two distinct frameworks. One was titled "A Framework for the Conclusion of a Peace Treaty between Egypt and Israel." It provided for a phased Israeli withdrawal from the Sinai and normalized relations between the two countries.

The other framework of the Camp David Accords pertained to Palestinian affairs and was titled "A Framework for Peace in the Middle East." Based on UN Security Council Resolution 242 from 1967, it was to provide the basis for a comprehensive settlement to the Arab-Israeli conflict and, therewith, also progress on the Palestinian issue. Palestinians were to be granted "full autonomy" after a five-year transition period during which they would elect a "self-governing authority." Negotiations toward the final status of the West Bank and Gaza would occur after the transition period.[11] Ironically, as much as Begin and Sadat disliked each other, a few months later, they would share a Nobel Peace Prize for the Accords.

To Palestinian leaders, however, the framework was nothing but a scheme to co-opt them into acquiescence. It was not clear what the term "autonomy" meant, but it was certainly not equal to sovereignty. Despite Sadat's Knesset speech, all along he had been distrusted by Palestinians and other Arabs for selling out to Israel. They were correct. The Egyptian President's commitment to Palestine was feeble at best, as was his commitment to pan-Arab causes. What mattered was his country's peace with Israel, as that would allow him to strengthen his ties with the U.S., thereby stabilizing Egypt and increasing his authority. His two-faced maneuvering was evident to other Arab leaders, who suspended Egypt from the Arab League. For some, such measures did not go far enough. On October 6, 1981, as Sadat was attending a parade in Cairo, a member of the Egyptian Islamic Jihad group shot and killed him.

Just a few weeks prior, Menachem Begin had been inaugurated for his second term as Israel's prime minister. Yitzhak Shamir continued as foreign minister, while Ariel Sharon became defense minister. It was an aggressively expansionist trio and thus displacements of Palestinians and settlement activity accelerated. When Begin first assumed office in 1977, the number of settlers in the West Bank was at about 4,400. By 1985, this number had increased tenfold, along with the establishment of almost seventy settlements.[12] To top things off, in 1980 Israel had also formalized the annexation of East Jerusalem in violation of international law.

For strategic and ideological reasons, the U.S. was acquiescing to Israeli expansionism. In early 1979, the Iranian Revolution had ousted the Iranian Shah, an important U.S. ally in the Middle East. At the end of the year, the Soviet Union invaded Afghanistan, and this further endangered U.S. control of the region and the oil flow from the Persian Gulf. These events increased Israel's strategic value as a reliable partner in the Middle East. All the while, fundamentalist Christian groups in the U.S. continued their lobbying efforts on behalf of Israeli expansionism. With the beginning of Ronald Reagan's presidency in 1981, their campaigns once again found very receptive ears. It was well known that Reagan himself, as well as several of his key aides, identified with supposed Biblical prophecies about the destiny of Jews in the Holy Land.

Escalation in Lebanon

While Israeli-Egyptian relations were improving, Lebanon was drawn increasingly into the Israeli-Palestinian conflict. Some historical background will be helpful here: Before the First World War, Lebanon had been part of Syria and was ruled by the Ottoman Empire. As we have seen in Chapter 3, when the Ottomans were defeated, France and Great Britain divvied up large parts of Ottoman/Arab lands. Lebanon fell under French influence, and it was only after the Second World War that the country became independent. In the 1970s, however, a variety of factors contributed to increasing societal conflict. The initial opponents were the so-called Lebanese National Movement (LNM), led by the Druze Kamal Jumblatt and supported by the Palestinians in the country.[13] Opposite them were Christian (Maronite) Phalange militias with a right-wing and sectarian commitment to their own dominance. They were led by Bashir Gemayel and supported by Israel, which favored a Christian-led country to its north rather than a Muslim-led one.

When, in April 1975, Phalange paramilitaries attacked a bus, killing over a dozen Palestinian passengers, the strife escalated into a civil war. Yet, it would get even messier. As the conflict unfolded, Syria deployed its forces, desiring to reassert its historical influence in Lebanon. Moreover, as we have seen above, the PLO had found refuge in southern Lebanon after it was forced to leave Jordan in 1970. The area it controlled was known as Fatahland and it had become a launching ground for attacks against Israel. In early 1978, the PLO hijacked an Israeli bus and murdered thirty-five Israeli civilians. The IDF retaliated with Operation Litani, an invasion of southern Lebanon to eradicate PLO bases. About 300 PLO fighters died, along with hundreds of Palestinian and Lebanese civilians. Moreover, through the IDF's heavy bombing, hundreds of Lebanese homes were destroyed. The IDF lost eighteen soldiers.[14] In the aftermath, Israel armed and trained the Southern Lebanon Army, a Christian-led militia that contributed to simmering tensions.

Those tensions boiled over in the summer of 1982. In June, three Palestinian gunmen shot and wounded Israel's Ambassador in London outside the city's Dorchester Hotel as he was leaving a dinner event. Even though the act was not sanctioned by the PLO, Israel used the event as a pretense to an undertaking it had wanted all along. It was an opportunity to completely eliminate the organization in Lebanon, rout Syrian forces, and establish a new sphere of influence inside the borders of its northern neighbor. The military campaign was dubbed *Operation Peace for Galilee* and it was led by Ariel Sharon. On June 6, 1982, about 80,000 Israeli troops penetrated deep into Lebanon.[15] Once again, the IDF, with considerable U.S. help, was superiorly equipped vis-à-vis its enemies.

The PLO's guerilla fighters and the 40,000 Syrian troops did not stand a chance.[16] Syria was quick to accept a ceasefire, but Palestinians and their Lebanese allies were left to be beaten badly in the south as well during the IDF's siege of the Lebanese capital Beirut. As the siege affected hundreds of thousands of civilians, it led to considerable international criticism. On August 12, the U.S. brokered a truce, and subsequently a multinational peacekeeping force arrived to oversee the withdrawal of Israeli troops from Beirut and the PLO's departure from Lebanon. By late August, Arafat and several thousand Palestinian fighters left for Tunisia and various other Arab countries. Tunisia would now be the new PLO headquarters. Upon their departure, an estimated 19,000 Arabs were dead. Israel suffered about 370 casualties.[17]

However, for extremist Phalangist Christians, the score was not settled. Under the pretext that there were PLO fighters remaining in the Palestinian refugee camps of Sabra and Shatila, they requested permission from Ariel Sharon to enter the camps. He granted it and what unfolded then was horrific. Wandering the streets, the Phalangists brutally massacred between hundreds and 3,500 (estimates vary widely) individuals, mostly civilians, including many women and children.[18] It should be noted that while this incident was, by far, the most horrendous assault during the war, there was also mass violence against Christians, notably in early 1976 at Damour, where hundreds of civilians were killed.[19] This massacre, in turn, was the revenge for an earlier massacre on Muslims in a Muslim neighborhood of East Beirut.

In May 1983, Israel and Lebanon signed a security agreement, providing for the Israeli withdrawal from Lebanon. However, to protect its northern towns and settlements, IDF forces remained within Lebanese borders in the country's very south. With the PLO gone, its enemy now was the newly formed pro-Syrian and Iranian Shi'ite militia *Hezbollah* (Party of God). As the general volatility within the country continued, Israel and the U.S. were intent on securing advantages for the Maronites. In April, the American embassy had been bombed in resentment, killing dozens of individuals and now, as American military positions were attacked, the White House ordered counterattacks, resulting in numerous casualties. Retaliation came in the form of suicide bombing attacks of the marine barracks at the Beirut International Airport in October 1983, killing 241 American service-members, dozens of French military personnel, and some civilians. In early 1984, American troops left Lebanon.[20]

The political situation in Israel was also evolving. After the Sabra and Shatila massacre, an Israeli investigation concluded that the IDF and political leaders bore indirect responsibility as they turned a blind eye to the killings. Ariel Sharon quit his post, and Menachem Begin became an exhausted and depressed man, ultimately resigning in August 1983. He was succeeded by Yitzhak Shamir. The Likud party was politically damaged and unable to form a government on its own. The July 1984 election thus led to a national unity government with the Likud and Labor parties forming a government together. Each party would provide the prime minister for a two-year term. Labor's Shimon Peres was prime minister and Likud's Yitzhak Shamir was foreign minister until October 1986, whereupon they would switch positions.

The First Intifada

The Lebanon War had illustrated just how easily the U.S. could be drawn into perilous situations in the region. Thus, President Reagan intended to resume a political process toward resolving the Israeli-Palestinian conflict. On September 1, 1982, the administration published a plan that entailed the freezing of Jewish settlements and the establishment of an autonomous Palestine, federated with Jordan. The plan did not foresee any sovereignty for Palestinians and was therefore unacceptable to them. On the Israeli side, surrendering the West Bank to Palestinians was unthinkable to the Likud government. In short, the plan was a non-starter.

The next initiative came from the government of Saudi Arabia and was adopted by a group of Arab leaders on September 9, 1982 in the

Moroccan city of Fez. Named after the conference site, the Fez Plan was based on UN Security Council Resolution 242 and called for Israel's withdrawal from Palestinian territories occupied since 1967, the removal of Jewish settlements in these territories, and the establishment of a PLO-led Palestinian state. Again, Israel rejected the plan outright.[21]

Meanwhile, the Israeli occupation of Palestinian lands was about to enter its third decade, and it was only worsening. With Defense Minister Yitzhak Rabin's so-called "iron fist" approach, the daily experience for Palestinians now included an increasing number of detentions, deportations, house demolitions, and expropriations. On December 8, 1987, a spark was ignited that would lead to a larger confrontation. Near a checkpoint at the Gaza Strip, an IDF truck hit a group of Palestinians, killing four of them. It was disputed whether this was an accident or intentional. In any case, when a crowd of Palestinians gathered the next morning to lament their deaths and express their anger, Israeli forces shot and killed a juvenile protestor.

Within days the Gaza Strip and the West Bank were in the pangs of a mass uprising not seen since the 1936 Arab Revolt discussed in Chapter 3. It was referred to as an *Intifada*, which is Arabic for "shaking off," meaning shaking off the occupation. It was coordinated by student, political, professional, and neighborhood groups, which, in turn, were led by the Unified National Leadership (UNL). The UNL's demand was the creation of an independent PLO-led state, which was to coexist with Israel. Tactics included acts of civil resistance such as strikes, protests, and tax boycotts, but there were also stones and Molotov cocktails being thrown at Israeli soldiers and property. The IDF responded with armored vehicles, tear gas, rubber bullets, and assault rifles. The difference in the weaponry on each side was, once again, illustrative of the power imbalance between the Palestinians and Israel.

The Intifada largely resembled an anti-colonial struggle and as it was unfolding, Islamic charities and welfare organizations were spreading. They provided much-needed medical relief as well as educational and social services. Islamic political organizations soon followed suit. For decades, Palestinians had witnessed the failure of their secular leaderships; the new Islamic organizations, foremost Hamas and Islamic Jihad, gave them new hope. Hamas is the better-known organization. Its leader was a wheelchair-bound and nearly blind man named Sheikh Ahmed Yassin. In 1948 he and his family were forced to flee the village of al-Jura, which was destroyed and then supplanted by the Israeli city of Ashkelon. Hamas is an acronym for *Harakat al-Muqawama al-Islamiya*, or Islamic Resistance Movement. The word Hamas translates into zeal and bravery. Hamas rejected Israel's legitimacy and explained its reasoning as follows:

> Hamas is a popular struggle movement that seeks to liberate Palestine in its entirety from the Mediterranean Sea to the River Jordan ... The Palestinian people are the direct target of the Zionist settler occupation. Therefore, they must bear the main burden of resisting the unjust occupation. This is why Hamas seeks to mobilize the full potential of the Palestinian people and channel it into steadfast resistance against the usurper.[22]

In due time, Israel, the U.S., and the EU would designate Hamas as a terrorist organization. Meanwhile, in Israel, the 1988 elections enabled Likud to form a majority coalition without Labor. Yitzhak Shamir remained prime minister and Israel's "iron fist" approach hardened further. Fighting on the streets continued as well, and the international audience took notice as images in the media showed Palestinian youth with slingshots being confronted by Israeli tanks and heavily equipped soldiers, who were instructed to break the bones of stone-throwing children.

Perhaps for the first time in the history of the conflict, Israel's image was tainted. At its November meeting, the UN General Assembly voted to condemn Israeli violations of human rights as well as Israeli activities in the Occupied Territories. The Intifada would come to last until the beginning of the 1990s. Ultimately, it would contribute to the emergence of negotiations between the two sides, but Palestinians paid a heavy price for their resistance. More than 1,000 Palestinians were killed by the IDF and tens of thousands were wounded. On the Israeli side there were about 150 dead, a significant portion of them civilians.[23]

Conclusion

After the humiliation of the 1967 War, Arabs were hoping for some redemption in the 1973 War. Yet, Israel enjoyed such military superiority over Arab forces that it not only won the war but could now remain seemingly indefinitely on the territories beyond the 1967 lines. A few years later, Menachem Begin thus declared at the graveside of Ze'ev Jabotinsky that the land was now "entirely under our control" and he promised, "It will never again be divided."[24] What followed were massive settlement programs on Palestinian lands, consistently hindering the emergence of a Palestinian state. Indeed, by the year 1990, there would be nearly 80,000 Jewish settlers on Palestinian lands.[25]

Like previous chapters, this chapter again illustrated Thucydides' dictum that "the strong do what they have the power to do." The second part of this dictum, "and the weak accept what they have to accept," once again did not bear out in a straightforward way. In this historical episode we saw that Palestinians continued to engage in civil and armed resistance and violence, including against civilians. It is important to note here that armed resistance against an occupying force is legal under international law. Targeting civilians, however, is, of course, not. While Palestinian groups have doubtlessly targeted civilians over the years, so has Israel. In fact, the latter has done so to an incomparably higher extent. A simple look at civilian casualty numbers in any given escalation or over time demonstrates this compellingly.

Suggested Further Readings

Alterman, Eric. 2022. *We Are Not One: A History of America's Fight Over Israel*. New York: Basic Books.

Anziska, Seth. 2018. *Preventing Palestine: A Political History from Camp David to Oslo*. Princeton, NJ: Princeton University Press.

Hart, Alan. 1989. *Arafat: A Political Biography*. Bloomington, IN: Indiana University Press.

Hirst, David. 2003. *The Gun and the Olive Branch*, 3rd edition. New York: Thunder's Mouth Press.

Quandt. William 1986. *Camp David*. Washington, DC: Brookings University Press.

Wright, Lawrence. 2014. *Thirteen Days in September: Carter, Begin, and Sadat at Camp David*. New York: Alfred Knopf.

Notes

1 Charles Smith. 2004. *Palestine and the Arab-Israeli Conflict*, 5th edition. New York: Bedford/St. Martin's, p. 307; Benny Morris. 1999. *Righteous Victims*. New York: Alfred Knopf, pp. 354–357; Mark Tessler. 2009. *A History of the Israeli-Palestinian Conflict*. Bloomington, IN: Indiana University Press, p. 449.

2 Benny Morris, *Righteous Victims*, pp. 367–369; David Lesch. 2008. *The Arab-Israeli Conflict*. New York: Oxford University Press, p. 235.

3 Ian Black. 2017. *Enemies and Neighbors: Arabs and Jews in Palestine and Israel, 1917–2017*. New York: Atlantic Monthly Press, p. 219.

4 Nadav Safran. 1977. "Trial by Ordeal: The Yom Kippur War, October 1973." *International Security* 2: 133–170; David Lesch, *The Arab-Israeli Conflict*, pp. 236–243; Benny Morris, *Righteous Victims*, pp. 390, 396, and 434.

5 Ian Black, *Enemies and Neighbors*, p. 226; David Lesch, *The Arab-Israeli-Conflict*, pp. 247–248; Mark Tessler, *A History of the Israeli-Palestinian Conflict*, p. 476.

6 David Lesch, *The Arab-Israeli-Conflict*, pp. 247–248; Mark Tessler, *A History of the Israeli-Palestinian Conflict*, p. 476.

7 Richard Parker, ed. 2001. *The October War*. Gainesville, FL: University of Florida Press, p. 9; Trevor Dupuy. 1978. *Elusive Victory: The Arab-Israeli Wars, 1947–1974*. New York: Harper & Row, p. 609.

8 These are UN General Assembly Resolutions 3237 and 3236, respectively.
9 Quoted in Colin Shindler. 1995. *Israel, Likud and the Zionist Dream*. London: I.B. Taurus & Co, p. 85. (brackets are added).
10 Avi Shlaim. 2014. *The Iron Wall*. New York: W.W. Norton, p. 362; Rashid Khalidi. 2020. *The Hundred Years' War on Palestine*. New York: Metropolitan Books, p. 135.
11 David Lesch, *The Arab-Israel-War*, p. 263; Avi Shlaim, *The Iron Wall*, p. 383; Ian Black, *Enemies and Neighbors*, p. 246.
12 Silvan Hirsch-Hoefler and Cas Mudde. 2020. *The Israeli Settler Movement*. New York: Cambridge University Press, pp. 47–48.
13 David Lesch, *The Arab-Israeli Conflict*, p. 289.
14 Benny Morris, *Righteous Victims*, p. 501.
15 Mark Tessler, *A History of the Israeli-Palestinian Conflict*, p. 574.
16 David Lesch, *The Arab-Israeli Conflict*, p. 294.
17 Ibrahim Abu-Lughod and Eqbal Ahmad. 1983. "The 1982 Israeli Invasion of Lebanon: The Casualties." *Race & Class* 24: 340–343.
18 Ibrahim Abu-Lughod and Eqbal Ahmad, "The 1982 Israeli Invasion of Lebanon," pp. 340–343.
19 Rashid Khalidi, *The Hundred Years' War*, p. 128.
20 Charles Smith, *Palestine and the Arab-Israeli Conflict*, p. 371; Mark Tessler, *A History of the Israeli-Palestinian Conflict*, pp. 624, 630, and 631.
21 Charles Smith, *Palestine and the Arab-Israeli Conflict*, pp. 368–369; David Lesch, *The Arab-Israeli Conflict*, p. 295.
22 James Gelvin. 2014. *The Israel-Palestine Conflict*. Cambridge: Cambridge University Press, p. 226; see also Muhammad Maqdsi. 1993. "Charter of the Islamic Resistance Movement (Hamas) of Palestine." *Journal of Palestine Studies* 22: 122–134.
23 The Israeli Information Center for Human Rights in the Occupied Territories. *Fatalities in the First Intifada*. Available at www.btselem.org/statistics/first_intifada_tables
24 Quoted in Avi Shlaim, *The Iron Wall*, p. 401.
25 Silvan Hirsch-Hoefler and Cas Mudde, *The Israeli Settler Movement*, p. 48.

6 Peace Process to Nowhere

Yitzhak Rabin was born in 1922 in Jerusalem, where his parents had emigrated to from the East European Pale of Settlement just a few years earlier. In his youth, Rabin aspired to be an engineer, possibly studying at Berkeley. His life took a fundamentally different turn, however, when, as a teenager, he acquired his first military experiences with the Haganah, the Yishuv's militia. His passion for furthering the Jewish national cause intensified during the Arab Revolt of the late 1930s, and in the 1948 War, he led several Jewish operations. Among them were the expulsion of about 50,000 Palestinians from the towns of Ramle and Lydda. In 1964, Rabin was named the Israeli Defense Forces' Chief of Staff, and in the 1967 War, he led his troops to a stunning victory.

After the 1967 War, Rabin began a career in politics. His first post was a five-year ambassadorship in the U.S. In 1974, he rose to the premiership of Israel when he succeeded Golda Meir as prime minister. Notably, he was the first Israeli prime minister who was born in what had been Palestine but was now Israel. He was also the first prime minister to come from the ranks of the military. For the better part of the 1980s, Rabin served as defense minister and then again as prime minister in 1992. His greatest political achievement was the signing of the Oslo Accords in 1993. A year later, together with Shimon Peres and Yasir Arafat, he was awarded the Nobel Peace Prize.

New Attempts at Diplomacy

As the 1980s progressed, the PLO faced the possibility that their armed struggle was wholly ineffective against the preponderant power of Israel. A Palestinian state in Gaza and the West Bank with East Jerusalem as its capital might well be the best they could achieve. In November 1988, the Palestinian National Council met in Algiers and formalized its new position in a declaration of independence. It accepted partition as well as

DOI: 10.4324/9781003536260-6

UN Security Council Resolutions 242 and 338, and disavowed armed struggle. This became known as the PLO's "historic compromise." It was indeed a profound statement, not only in that the PLO now accepted the existence of Israel, but also that Palestinians should own only the 22 percent of a land that not long ago had been entirely theirs.

For the U.S., in the meantime, the Cold War was winding down and, with the PLO's acceptance of Israel, the new administration of George H. W. Bush showed a new willingness to help toward a resolution of the long-running conflict. It was a startling moment when, in May 1989, Secretary of State James Baker spoke at the convention of the influential American Israel Public Affairs Committee (AIPAC) and asked Israeli leaders to discard visions of a Greater Israel, to stop annexations and settlements, and to recognize Palestinians' political rights. Israel, however, was not willing to give even "one inch" of the land, as Prime Minister Shamir put it. The construction of new settlements in the Occupied Territories continued unabated. In 1990, the number of settlers increased by 8,600, and in following years, they increased by 10,000 or more every year.[1]

A concrete attempt to break the impasse occurred in October 1991 when the U.S. initiated the Middle East Peace Conference to convene in Madrid. It pledged to act as an "honest broker" between Israel, Syria, Lebanon, Jordan, and the Palestinians.[2] This quickly turned out to be an empty promise, however, as the U.S. accepted Israel's demand to not allow Palestinians to have their own delegation; they had to be part of the Jordanian delegation. Of further humiliation to Palestinians was that Israel was successful in rejecting critical issues for Palestinians on the agenda. The issues of refugees, the future of Jerusalem, and Palestinian sovereignty over their own lands were all not to be part of the discussion. After Madrid, as the talks continued in Washington, it seemed that these were really just a stalling tactic toward building more and more settlements.

The Oslo Accords

A new opportunity arose after the 1992 Israeli elections. The Intifada had been raging for five years and growing swaths of the Israeli public came to consider the continued occupation too costly. How to handle it became a major point of debate between the ruling Likud and the contending Labor Party. Both Likud and Labor leaders agreed on the Zionist aspiration for an expansion of the Jewish state. Where they differed was that the latter were willing to make some political and territorial concessions in order to reduce the cost of the occupation and to avoid demographically undermining the Jewish state. The electorate chose

Labor, and on July 13, Yitzhak Rabin became the new prime minister, claiming simultaneously the defense minister post. Shimon Peres was appointed as foreign minister.

The Washington talks had gone nowhere and so, under strict secrecy, the new government decided to do something that had been completely taboo: Hold direct talks with the PLO. Interestingly, these occurred in Oslo because Norway had offered itself as a mediator to the conflicting parties. It was an opportune moment for the Israelis. Arafat and the PLO were said to be on the ropes, as the popularity of Hamas and Islamic Jihad was rising. The expectation was that this would make him willing to offer far-reaching concessions.

Having begun in January 1993, the talks lasted eight months. They culminated in an exchange of letters of mutual recognition and the Deceleration of Principles (DOP), commonly referred to as the Oslo Accords. Arafat's letter to Yitzhak Rabin from September 9, 1993 read as follows:

> Mr. Prime Minister, ... The PLO recognizes the right of the State of Israel to exist in peace and security. The PLO accepts United Nations Security Council Resolution 242 and 338. The PLO commits itself to the Middle East peace process and to a peaceful resolution of the conflict between the two sides and declares that all outstanding issues relating to permanent status will be resolved through negotiations. ... [T]he PLO renounces the use of terrorism and other acts of violence ...[3]

Rabin's letter to Arafat was much shorter:

> Mr. Chairman, ... I wish to inform you that ... the Government of Israel has decided to recognize the PLO as the representative of the Palestinian people and commence negotiations with the PLO within the Middle East peace process.

Notably, while the PLO recognized Israel's right to exist, Rabin offered no such pledge for a Palestinian state. Some of the DOP's specifics stipulated that within three months, the IDF was to withdraw from the Gaza Strip and the Jericho area. By July 1994, elections would establish the Palestinian Authority (PA) as a new governing body. Subsequently, Israeli and Palestinian leaders would enter into final status negotiations, which were to conclude by the summer of 1999. These would address the status of Jerusalem, the rights of refugees, Jewish settlements in the occupied territories, and the delineation of final borders. On September

13, 1993, U.S. President Bill Clinton hosted Rabin and Arafat in Washington. With the world watching the festively dressed event on the White House lawn, the Accords were signed.[4]

After the Oslo Accords, PLO leaders returned from their Tunisian exile to the Occupied Territories, where they faced immediate criticism. Indeed, the Accords seemed to be very disadvantageous to Palestinians. The PA would have limited authority only, namely in realms such as education, culture, health, and social welfare. According to the DOP, Palestinians could also not protect themselves from IDF assaults or Jewish settlers, and they would have no control over their own movement into and out of their territory. On a more fundamental level, the PLO was criticized for having conceded to a reframing of the conflict. So far, it had defined the struggle as one against settler-colonial subjugation. Now, however, the conflict was framed as a contest between two supposedly equal contenders while concealing the tremendous power imbalance between them.[5]

In September 1995, two years after their first meeting, Arafat and Rabin met again on the White House lawn and signed interim agreements which came to be known simply as Oslo II. As illustrated in Map 6.1, it divided the Palestinian territories into a patchwork of areas – A, B, and C. Area A comprised 18 percent of the territory, and here the PA was granted civilian and security authority. It included the West Bank cities of Jericho, Qalqilya, Ramallah, Bethlehem, Jenin, Nablus, Tulkram, and part of Hebron. In Area B, which comprised 22 percent of the territory and included more than 400 villages and their surrounding areas, the PA attained civilian authority (security authority was to be shared between the PA and Israel). Area C comprised over 60 percent of the land and was placed under complete Israeli authority. It included almost all of the Jewish settlements. Areas A and B were home to nearly 90 percent of the Palestinian population.[6] While Israeli withdrawal from these areas was to take place in the near term, the withdrawal from Area C would be dependent on the conclusion of permanent status negotiations.

Notably, neither Oslo I nor Oslo II guaranteed statehood for Palestinians. Israel retained almost full control over any access to and exit from the Occupied Territories. Israel was also to control a major part of Palestinian revenues coming from taxes. The PA's major function was henceforth the administrative management of towns and villages, running schools and health services, maintaining utilities and the like. Ironically, it also came to be responsible for the safety of illegal Jewish settlers against any possible resistance.[7] Hamas and the Islamic Jihad were not alone in accusing the PLO of betraying the Palestinian cause. While, initially, many Palestinians were optimistic that Oslo was a

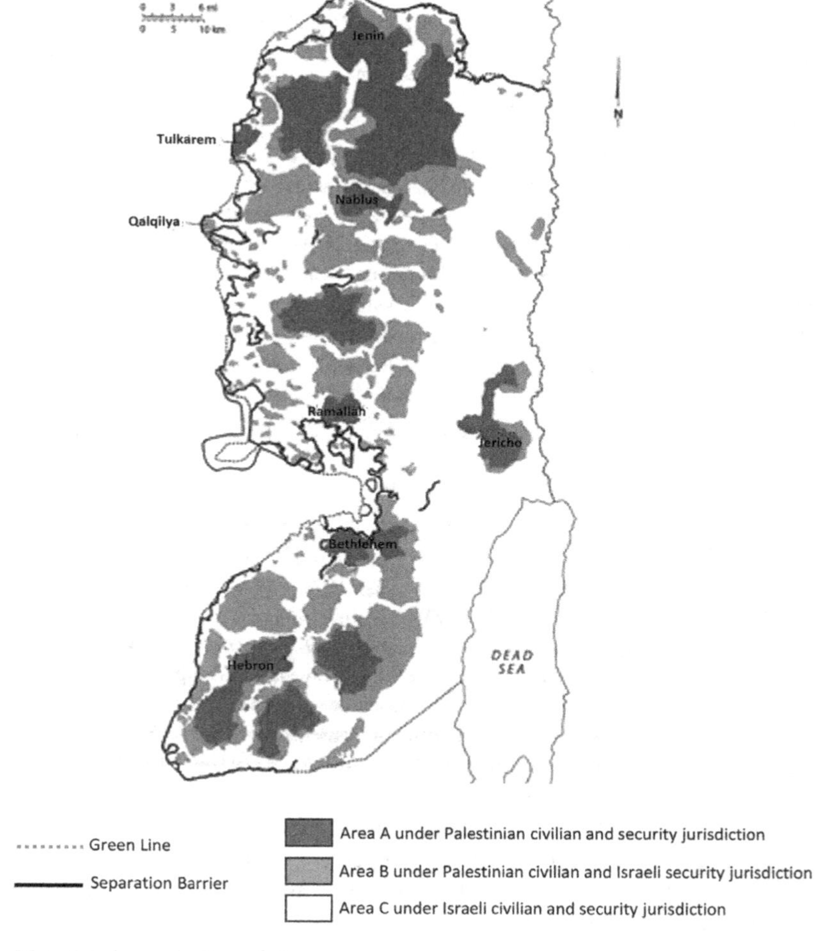

Map 6.1 Areas A, B, and C
Source: Adapted version of a map from Gershon Shafir. 2017. *A Half Century of Occupation*. Oakland, CA: University of California Press, p. 45. Used with permission.

stepping stone toward a Palestinian state, ultimately, they came to see it as an American–Israeli ruse. It was judged to be a historic mistake, even a capitulation.

In October, Rabin presented the Oslo II agreement to the Israeli Knesset. He assured the lawmakers that Israel would not return to the Green Line, even though this was required under international law. The Palestinian "entity" that would result from Oslo II would be something "less than a state," and all of Jerusalem would remain under Israeli sovereignty.[8] Although the Oslo process was clearly a win for Israel, Rabin faced harsh criticism. The small concessions he made toward the PA's administrative authorities in limited areas of the Occupied Territories led the Likud party as well as the settler movement *Gush Emunim* (Bloc of the Faithful) to accuse him of surrendering what they called Eretz Yisrael. A little more than a month after Rabin signed the Oslo II agreement, a Jewish extremist assassinated him during a public rally at Tel Aviv's King of Israel Square.

From Oslo to Deadlock

Extremists and fanatical Jewish settlers and extremists had been intent on derailing the Oslo process all along. Among the best-known examples is the former New York physician Baruch Goldstein's February 1994 murder of twenty-nine Palestinian worshippers in Hebron's Ibrahimi Mosque, a site that Jews refer to as the Cave of Machpelah. He carried out his deed on the Jewish Purim holiday, which in this year was also the third Friday of the holy month of Ramadan for Muslims. Palestinian extremism also returned, now often in the form of Hamas suicide attacks in Israeli cities and on buses, causing many civilian fatalities. For people around the world these acts came to be the main characteristic of the organization. Arafat was either unable or unwilling to halt them.

The deteriorating security situation facilitated the renewed rise of the more aggressive Likud, and in June 1996, Benjamin Netanyahu assumed the premiership. His election did not bode well for the prospect of any progress. Netanyahu was raised in a Revisionist Zionist household and viewed Israel's relations with its Arab neighbors to be doomed to permanent conflict. A few years earlier, he had written a book titled *A Place Among the Nations: Israel and the World*. To a considerable extent, it is an account of his negative view of Arabs, their history, and their culture. Just a few months after he took office, Netanyahu proclaimed that there would never be a Palestinian state between the Mediterranean Sea and the Jordan River.

In the years to come, the Netanyahu government worked not only on derailing the Oslo process but also on the realization of a Greater Israel. By the end of the decade, there would be about twice as many settlements as there were at the beginning of the peace process.[9]

Along with settlements came so-called bypass roads which connected settlements to each other and to Israel. The Israeli army often referred to these as "sterile roads" as no Palestinians were allowed on them. Not surprisingly, they have also been referred to as apartheid roads. While they facilitated the commutes of Jews, they restricted the movement of Palestinians. But even more significant was that they increasingly hindered the eventual realization of a contiguous Palestinian state.

Indeed, as the end of the decade approached, it was increasingly clear that the Oslo process would not lead to a Palestinian state. Through all the years, the PA had acquired jurisdiction over only some 40 percent of the West Bank, including Gaza, but excluding East Jerusalem. Netanyahu, so it seemed, had succeeded in halting the peace process. This outlook, however, was not to the liking of the Israeli populace, especially the left, which, at this time, favored some settlement with the Palestinians. Moreover, Netanyahu's leadership worsened Israel's economic situation, and the country became plagued by rising ethnic divisions.

A small glimmer of hope emerged when Ehud Barak from the Labor Party won the 1999 elections. Barak was a distinguished military veteran and he carried a reputation for political pragmatism. Notably, some years after his premiership, he acknowledged that Israel, with its oppression of Palestinians, was heading down a path toward becoming an apartheid state. He may have already realized this when he was leading the country as he was intent on reaching a final resolution. In any case, Barak asked the American President Bill Clinton to facilitate a summit. Clinton, intent on the peace process being his chief international legacy, agreed to host it at Maryland's Camp David.

Arafat found himself in a dilemma. He was convinced that any Israeli proposal would fall short of Palestinian expectations and was thus disinclined to participate. At the same time, he feared that if he declined the invitation, he would be portrayed as an obstructionist by the international community. In the end, after obtaining Clinton's personal assurance that he would not be blamed for a possible failure, Arafat agreed to attend. The meeting began on July 11, 2000 and lasted for fifteen days. Reminiscent of the year 1978, when the Egyptian President Sadat met with the Israeli Premier Menachem Begin, this meeting at Camp David was also filled with much tension. Arafat fundamentally mistrusted Barak, and Barak carried open contempt for Arafat.[10]

The process and the outcome of the meeting are difficult to reconstruct because they are plagued by contradictory testimonies. Barak, it seems, offered Arafat about 92 percent of the West Bank while retaining the vast majority of settlements. Together with the bypass roads, this left no contiguous state for the Palestinians. Furthermore, Barak proposed the creation of two capitals: Jerusalem would be Israel's capital and "al-Quds" would be Palestine's. It was a disingenuous move. While al-Quds is the Arabic name for Jerusalem, what Barak was in fact referring to was a village on the outskirts of East Jerusalem. Moreover, Palestinians were to surrender any claim to a right of return, accept Israeli military posts in the Jordan Valley, and agree to Israeli control over its borders.[11]

Barak's proposal was widely hailed as very generous. When compared to previous Israeli offers, this may indeed be true. However, it is certainly not true when measured against what Palestinians had already lost and conceded to. Arafat rejected the proposal and made no counterproposal. On July 25 the summit broke up in failure. Contrary to his promise, Clinton did blame Arafat. However, some years later, Shlomo Ben-Ami, one of Israel's chief negotiators at Camp David, commented on an American news show, "If I were a Palestinian, I would have rejected Camp David as well."[12] Similarly, the American negotiator Aaron David Miller acknowledged that the summit was governed by "totally unrealistic expectations on what the Palestinians needed to close a deal."[13]

The Second Intifada

Despite the failure at Camp David, in late December 2000, just before leaving office, Bill Clinton made a final attempt to force an agreement. Known as the Clinton Parameters, Israel was to withdraw from about 95 percent of the Occupied Territories while most of the Jewish settlers would concentrate in the remaining 5 percent. Palestinians would be compensated with no more than 3 percent of Israeli territory. East Jerusalem would become the capital of the Palestinian state. Palestinians, moreover, would receive the Haram-al Sharif itself, while Israel would retain sovereignty over the Western Wall and the Jewish quarter in the Old City.[14]

The parameters were clearly closer to the Palestinian demands than what Barak had offered at Camp David. However, when Israeli and Palestinian delegations met in the Egyptian city of Taba to discuss them, they made no progress. The situation on the ground had changed in the meantime. On September 28, 2000, Likud party Leader Ariel Sharon, accompanied by hundreds of security personnel and media representatives, had ventured to the Haram al-Sharif/Temple Mount. Aiming to claim Jewish rights to the site, the act represented a serious affront to

Palestinians who saw their sacred area being violated. Sharon's venture quickly led to clashes between Palestinians and Israeli soldiers; it marked the beginning of the second Palestinian uprising, often referred to as the Al-Aqsa Intifada.

As the IDF used deadly force, Palestinians took to arms and explosives. A serious escalation was underway. Israel responded with helicopters, tanks, artillery, and even F-16 jets. Palestinians resorted to over two dozen suicide bombings, and Hamas and Islamic Jihad launched rockets into Israel. Soon, Fatah joined in as well. It was a catastrophic situation, and the casualty rates are telling. The second Intifada was shorter than the first Intifada. However, while during the first Intifada, well over 1,000 people were killed, the second one, petering out in 2005, claimed the lives of over 4,000. Of these, more than 3,000 were Palestinians and about 1,000 were Israelis; the majority of all these casualties were civilians.[15]

The onset of the second Intifada hardened the fronts yet further, and in March 2001, it helped Ariel Sharon become Israel's new prime minister. It didn't bode well for the future of Israeli-Palestinian relations. During his campaign, Sharon had declared the Oslo Accords invalid. He categorically opposed the evacuations of any settlements, a withdrawal from the Jordan Valley, and any concessions on Jerusalem. In fact, early on he demonstrated his intention to annex Jewish settlements along the Green Line, and to leave less than 50 percent of the West Bank for Palestinians.[16]

Just a few weeks earlier, Republican George W. Bush had assumed the U.S. presidency. Along with him, a class of so-called neoconservatives entered the White House. These were individuals who wanted to use the preponderance of U.S. military power toward a very active global role. With regard to the Middle East, they wanted to remake it so it would be more amenable to U.S. interests. For strategic and ideational reasons, these neoconservatives were also strongly pro-Israel. As a born-again Christian, President Bush brought his own religious predilections into office, and it showed in much of his rhetoric. He had personal sympathies for Sharon. Known as "The Bulldozer" in the conflict-ridden region, Bush referred to Sharon as a "man of peace."

Then came the horrific 9/11 attacks, appearing to validate the neoconservative worldview of a clash of civilizations that had been cultivated in the West for many decades, if not centuries. In this narrative the Islamic world is cast as an inevitable enemy to the Western world, a portrayal that would have serious consequences for Palestinians. The attacks had been committed by Al-Qaeda, an organization that was unrelated to the Palestinian Hamas or Islamic Jihad. Yet, in the public rhetoric of neoconservative leaders, all these and other so-called Islamist organizations were cut from the same cloth. In the Bush administration's subsequent War on Terror, all Islamist organizations had to be confronted and eliminated.

Global perception of Arafat and the PLO worsened yet further when, in early 2002, the Israeli Navy stopped the *Karin A* in the Red Sea. The ship was carrying a large load of lethal weapons from Iran to Gaza, including rockets, mortar shells, and antitank missiles. Arafat denied any relation between the PLO and the shipment, but he was not credible. At the same time, Palestinian suicide attacks were increasing with many Israel casualties. A large attack occurred on the evening of March 27 when a Hamas operative ignited his explosive belt in the Netanya Park Hotel during the Jewish Seder dinner to celebrate Passover. Thirty guests were killed and close to 150 were injured.[17]

The IDF had already been engaged in the West Bank, but the Netanya attack brought things to a head with Israel launching Operation Defensive Shield. It was the largest IDF operation in the West Bank since the 1967 War. Employing tanks, helicopters, and fighter jets, the goal was not only to destroy resistance bases but also to reestablish the deterrent power of the IDF. The Intifada was to be put out and never initiated again. The IDF moved to reoccupy the entire West Bank and surrounded Arafat's Ramallah compound, the *Muqataa*. The PA ceased its capability to function, and the already meager Palestinian economy and social services almost came to a complete halt. In the four months between the end of February and the end of June, nearly 500 Palestinians were killed, many of them civilians and at least seventy minors. On the Israeli side, there were more than 250 casualties, most of them civilians and including more than thirty children.[18]

As the violence was escalating, Saudi Arabia launched a new initiative at the Arab League's March meeting in Beirut. According to the plan, known as the Arab Peace Initiative, a sovereign Palestinian state was to be established on the 1967 lines. In return for Israel's withdrawal from the Occupied Territories, all twenty-one members of the League would sign a peace agreement with Israel and grant it full diplomatic recognition. In effect, the proposal reversed the "three nos" from the 1967 Khartoum Summit mentioned in Chapter 4. The plan could lead to sweeping change in the region; Israel would enjoy peace not only with its immediate Arab neighbors but with all of them. As a further important concession to Israel, the plan called for a just solution to the issue of Palestinian refugees, but it did not insist on a categorical right of return for all of them.

For the Sharon government, however, a withdrawal to the 1967 lines was a non-starter, and it rejected the plan out of hand. Soon after, the U. S. headed its initiative, which included Russia, the UN, and the EU, a group dubbed the "Quartet." The U.S. took the lead in authoring what came to be referred as the "Road Map." It included a set of measures that the conflicting sides would have to undertake simultaneously. Chief among them was that within the next two years, Israel was to halt its settlement activities while Palestinians were to halt all violence. By 2005, negotiations would be resumed toward a resolution of permanent status issues. To support this outcome, the Bush administration demanded a new Palestinian leadership. Arafat not only conceded to the plan, but also, surprisingly, created the new position of a prime minister. He appointed Mahmoud Abbas to fill the new role.

The Sharon government, however, after having demanded dozens of changes to the plan, violated its most fundamental requirement, namely the cessation of settlement expansions.[19] In the end, it is fair to say that what impeded both the Arab League's plan as well as the Quartet's was that, in the words of the historian Avi Shlaim, "Likud's ideology of a Greater Israel was simply incompatible with a genuine two-state solution."[20]

The Rise of Hamas

Amid international initiatives to bring forth a resolution, the Sharon government embarked upon building an enormous land barrier between Israel and the West Bank. It was to be hundreds of miles long and would often run east of the Green Line, that is, inside the Occupied Territories. It consisted of fences, barbed wire, and trenches, and in urban areas an enormous concrete wall. The effects on Palestinians were devastating. Their houses were demolished and their fields were lost.[21] The UN General Assembly protested the barrier, and in July 2004, the International Court of Justice (ICJ, sometimes referred to as the World Court) judged it to be in violation of international law, as it amounted to an annexation of Palestinian lands. Construction of the barrier continued unabated, however, as did settlement activity. By the end of 2007, the Jewish population in the West Bank was well over a quarter of a million.[22]

Strengthening Israel's hold on the West Bank was Sharon's main objective, and toward this end, he was willing to withdraw troops and settlements from Gaza. This, however, was not a concession to Palestinians. Gaza was a small and peripheral land strip that didn't have the emotional meaning for Jews as the West Bank did, and the cost of providing security for settlements there was just too high. However, to the international public, the act would be presented as one of goodwill, which in turn, Sharon hoped, would freeze the political process toward a Palestinian state. Thus, by mid-September 2005, Jewish settlers and soldiers were all evacuated. The land strip remained occupied, however, as Israel controlled all of its land border to Israel, its air space, territorial waters, and electricity and water supplies.

Shortly afterwards, in a puzzling move, Sharon withdrew from the Likud party and founded the Kadima (Forward) Party. In January 2006, however, he suffered a stroke and fell into a coma, a state in which he remained until his death in January 2014. Upon his stroke, he was succeeded by his party colleague Ehud Olmert. An even more monumental change had occurred on the Palestinian side just over a year earlier. At the end of October 2004, Arafat was emergency evacuated from Ramallah to a hospital in Paris, France. His ailment was mysterious; it was suspected that he had been poisoned. A few days later, on November 11, he died. An era had come to an end. While many grieved the man who had stood at the helm of the Palestinian cause for decades, others were relieved as they felt a need for change.

Arafat's successor was Mahmoud Abbas. He had been a member of Fatah since the organization's more aggressive early days, but by now, he had adopted the behaviors of acquiescence, condemning, for example, armed resistance. He was amenable to the U.S. and Israel, but his acceptance among Palestinians was rather shaky. In the January 2006 elections, Abbas was intent on changing this. To his dismay, however, voters gave the most seats to Hamas. Interestingly, a trend toward Islamic parties occurred in countries across the region. Too many people had grown entirely frustrated by the corruption and unresponsiveness of their secular governments.

Israel, however, along with the U.S. and other Western powers not only refused to recognize Hamas' election, but they also withheld the PA's tax revenues as well as international donations, thus seriously impairing the PA's ability to govern. As Fatah and Hamas were quarrelling, the latter feared a U.S.-supported scheme to oust it and thus retreated to Gaza, where it has been governing since. In June 2007, it fired rockets into Israel to protest the ongoing blockade. Israel, in turn, declared it to be a "hostile territory" and tightened its blockade. Henceforth, a bare minimum of emergency goods would enter the strip and an already disastrous humanitarian situation worsened yet further. As residents were permitted to leave in exceptional cases only, Gaza, in effect, became what has often been described as an open-air prison. The UN declared the blockade to be tantamount to collective punishment and in violation of international law. Despite this declaration, the blockade continues into the present.

The Gaza Wars

Tensions between Gaza and Israel had already been escalating in serious ways since the beginning of the siege in 2006. On top of continuous rocket attacks into Israel, in mid-2006, Hamas had managed to capture the IDF Corporal Gilad Shalit. Israel responded with Operation Summer Rains, a series of air strikes combined with ground incursions. The year ended up being tremendously bloody. Overall, the IDF killed about 660 Palestinians, the vast majority in the Gaza Strip, with about half of them not involved in the hostilities, including dozens of minors. The IDF also destroyed nearly 300 homes and significant parts of Gaza's infrastructure. On the Israeli side, there were six soldiers and seventeen civilians dead.[23]

A few weeks after Israel's Operation Summer Rains, Lebanon's Hezbollah acted in solidarity with Hamas, launching attacks in the north. In an initial ambush, after crossing the border, the group killed eight IDF soldiers. Israel responded like it had in Gaza, with preponderant power. Over the thirty-four days of fighting, Israel launched thousands of strikes, while Hezbollah was limited to its primitive missiles. More than 1,100 Lebanese died, the vast majority of them civilians. Israel lost twelve IDF soldiers and forty-three civilians.[24]

Both Hamas and Hezbollah had been receiving material and ideological support from Iran and Syria. As the Bush administration saw Israel's fight against these groups as an extension of its own War on Terror, in mid-2007, it committed itself to maintaining Israel's power preponderance with a $30 billion aid package. Over $20 billion of this aid was to be spent on U.S.-produced weapons.[25] One year later, the U.S. Congress legally codified its commitment to total Israeli military superiority. It guaranteed that Israel had "the ability to counter and defeat any credible conventional military threat from any individual state or possible coalition of states or from non-state actors, while sustaining minimal damage and casualties, through the use of superior military means."[26]

Things would come to a head again on November 4, 2008, when Israeli soldiers killed six members of Hamas who were allegedly digging a tunnel into Israel.[27] Hamas retaliated by firing dozens of rockets into Israel. Israel responded by launching Operation Cast Lead, an enormous air campaign with nearly 3,000 sorties and about 100 tons of bombs dropped. Hamas' primitive rockets were no match.[28] When a ceasefire came into effect in mid-January, nearly 1,400 Palestinians had been killed, most of them, once again, civilians, including about 300 children. Electrical and water systems became dysfunctional as thousands of homes were either damaged or destroyed, leaving countless people homeless. On the Israeli side, the death toll was limited to six soldiers and three civilians.[29]

Just a few days after the ceasefire, Barack Obama was sworn in as the new American president. Considering the Bush administration's policy toward the Middle East a failure, Obama intended to take a new approach. In June 2009, he traveled first to Saudi Arabia and then to Egypt. At Cairo University he gave a much-noted speech asking for "a new beginning" between the U.S. and Muslims around the world. He also addressed the Israeli-Palestinian conflict and, as was a tradition for American presidents, he emphasized that the bonds between the U.S. and Israel were unbreakable. He acknowledged, however, the Palestinian people's "daily humiliations" under occupation and the refugees' "pain of dislocation." He described Israeli settlements as a threat to a two-state solution and pledged to work toward progress.[30]

The prospects were not promising, however. The Jewish settler population in the Occupied Territories had grown to nearly half a million in the meantime. In March, Benjamin Netanyahu returned to power, accompanied by the very hawkish Foreign Minister Avigdor Lieberman, an open advocate for annexation of Palestinian lands. Obama would have a tough time when, in the summer of 2010, he hosted talks between Netanyahu and Abbas in Washington. What was needed most was a prolonged moratorium on settlements to allow time for negotiations. Toward this end, Israel was offered a rather spectacular multi-billion-dollar incentives package, including twenty fighter jets. It was unsuccessful.[31]

At the end of the year, thousands of miles away from the Israeli-Palestinian conflict, a tragic event ignited what would become the Arab Uprisings (also referred to as the Arab Spring). It happened in the Tunisian town of Siddi Bouzzid. The vegetable vendor Mohammed Bouazizi, frustrated by authoritarian and arbitrary government practices, and being repeatedly denied a new sales license, set himself on fire in the town's center. His act spurned mass protests and the eventual ousting of President Zine El Abidene Ben Ali. From Tunisia, the protests spread to Egypt, Syria, and across the Arab world. Israeli leaders watched with concern. Various authoritarian leaders in these countries tended to be submissive to Washington's will and thereby accepting of Israel's doings toward Palestinians. The popular will in Arab countries, however, was in favor of Palestinians. In the eyes of Israeli leaders, the possible democratization of Arab countries bore negative consequences for Israel.

Mahmoud Abbas too was concerned about the Arab Uprisings as he dealt with his own legitimacy problems. His official term had expired in 2009 and for the last few years he had been ruling as an authoritarian. The PA's assembly had not met since 2007. Plagued by the destructive relationship between Fatah and Hamas, Palestinians demanded an end to their division. Abbas had serious reservations about Hamas, but the mounting pressure ultimately forced him to concede to Hamas' inclusion. Despite a series of meetings between the heads of Fatah and Hamas, the formation of a unified government remained elusive, however.

Internationally, Abbas' main goal was to gain recognition of Palestinian statehood at the UN. For such to be binding, it would have to occur in the UN Security Council where a U.S. veto was all but certain. In the UN General Assembly, however, only a simple majority would be needed to recognize Palestine as a "non-member observer" state. The U.S. also engaged in obstructionism here, but its efforts were defied on November 29, 2012, when Palestine was promoted to its new status. Incidentally, this coincided with the sixty-fifth anniversary of the UN's decision to partition Mandatory Palestine. The PA would now be able to request the International Criminal Court to pursue possible Israeli war crimes.

As the PA was making some diplomatic progress, once again the situation was about to go sour in Gaza, where the Israeli blockade had made life miserable. Simmering tensions were coming to a head with the Israeli assassination of a Hamas leader and the organization's rocket firings into Israel, a few of them reaching Jerusalem and Tel Aviv. On November 14, 2012, Israel launched Operation Pillar of Defense, an eight-day attack with an enormous number of air and artillery strikes on several targets, including rocket launchers, tunnels, weapons factories, and storage facilities. Palestinians launched nearly 1,700 rockets from the Gaza Strip, with a significant amount of these intercepted by the Israeli air defense system. The fighting ended with an Egyptian-mediated ceasefire on November 21. It resulted in the deaths of 167 Palestinians, most of whom had no part in the hostilities. Countless homes and infrastructure were destroyed or seriously damaged. On the Israeli side, two IDF soldiers and four civilians were killed.[32]

However, it wouldn't be long until the next escalation. In June 2014, Hamas operatives murdered three Israeli teenagers at a West Bank settlement. On July 8, the IDF responded with another large-scale military operation, Protective Edge. The longest and most destructive hostilities in Gaza since 1967, it was, once again, a barrage of airstrikes and shellings. Hamas, in turn, once again fired rockets into Israel, and the conflict escalated into a full-scale war lasting almost two months. In late August, a ceasefire was agreed upon, but by this time more than 2,200 Palestinians had been killed, the most casualties since the 1967 War. The vast majority of these were not part of the hostilities and among them were over 500 children. In addition to human casualties many thousands of Palestinian homes were destroyed. With over sixty soldiers and six civilians dead, Israel suffered its heaviest losses since the 2006 Lebanon War.[33] Escalations and clashes in Gaza would continue over the next several years.

Conclusion

In the 1980s, as the Israeli occupation continued, Palestinians resisted through the Intifada. They expressed their anger mostly by throwing stones, as they were facing one of the most powerful militaries in the world. Also in the second Intifada, as well as all the other conflicts reviewed in this chapter, Israel's opponents were all non-state actors, individuals and guerrilla groups. Although various of them were receiving weaponry from Iran and Syria, they were clearly no match for the IDF, one of the world's most powerful militaries. Once again, we saw that the strong did what they had the power to do. The weak, for their part, did not just lay down and accept their fate. They fought back through the Intifadas and on many other occasions.

The power imbalance is also illustrated through the casualty statistics we encountered in this chapter. Most often these were drawn from the Israeli human rights organization B'Tselem. From September 2000 until July 2014, this organization recorded 8,166 conflict-related casualties. Of these, 7,065 were Palestinian and 1,101 were Israeli. Expressed differently, about 87 percent of deaths have been Palestinian and about 13 percent Israeli.[34] This brings forth the question of justice again. Of course, one must mourn the loss of innocent lives on both sides. But the bleeding and dying in the Israeli-Palestinian conflict is exceptionally more prevalent on the Palestinian side.

Suggested Further Readings

Baconi, Tareq. 2018. *Hamas Contained: The Rise and Pacification of Palestinian Resistance*. Stanford, CA: Stanford University Press.

Bauck, Petter and Mohammed Omer, eds. 2017. *The Oslo Accords 1993–2013: A Critical Assessment*. New York: The American University in Cairo Press.

Beilin, Yossi. 2004. *The Path to Geneva*. New York: RDV Books.

Finkelstein, Norman. 2018. *Gaza: An Inquest into Its Martyrdom*. Oakland, CA: University of California Press.

Quandt. William. 2005. *Peace Process*, 3rd edition. Washington, DC: The Brookings Institution Press.

Roy, Sara. 2016. *The Gaza Strip: The Political Economy of De-development*. Washington, DC: Institute for Palestine Studies

Salieh, Afif. 2011. *The Peace Process: From Breakthrough to Breakdown*. London: Saqi Books.

Swisher, Clayton. 2004. *The Truth About Camp David*. New York: Nation Books

Notes

1 Silvan Hirsch-Hoefler and Cas Mudde. 2020. *The Israeli Settler Movement*. New York: Cambridge University Press, p. 49.
2 Rashid Khalidi. 2020. *The Hundred Years' War on Palestine*. New York: Metropolitan Books, pp. 186–187.
3 The letters can be found on the United Nation's website at www.un.org/unispal/document/auto-insert-205528/
4 Mark Tessler. 2009. *A History of the Israeli-Palestinian Conflict*. Bloomington, IN: Indiana University Press, pp. 755–761; Avi Shlaim. 2014. *The Iron Wall*. New York: W.W. Norton, pp. 530–541.
5 Noura Erakat. 2019. *Justice for Some*. Stanford, CA: Stanford University Press, pp. 166–167.
6 Rashid Khalidi, *The Hundred Years' War*, p. 202.
7 Rashid Khalidi, *The Hundred Years' War*, p. 202..
8 Rabin's speech is available at www.jewishvirtuallibrary.org/pm-rabin-speech-to-knesset-on-ratification-of-oslo-peace-accords
9 Noura Erakat, *Justice for Some*, p. 172.
10 Daniel Kurtzer et al. 2017. *The Peace Puzzle*. Ithaca, NY: Cornell University Press, p. 133.
11 Uri Avnery. 2008. *Israel's Vicious Cycle*, edited by Sara Powell. London: Pluto Press, p. 20.
12 The transcript can be found at www.democracynow.org/2006/2/14/fmr_israeli_foreign_minister_if_i
13 Aaron David Miller. 2020. *Lost in the Woods: A Camp David Retrospective*. Carnegie Endowment for International Peace (July 13). https://carnegieendowment.org/2020/07/13/lost-in-woods-camp-david-retrospective-pub-82287
14 David Lesch. 2008. *The Arab-Israeli Conflict*. New York: Oxford University Press, pp. 387–388; Khaled Elgindy. 2019. *Blind Spot: America and the Palestinians, from Balfour to Trump*. Washington, DC: Brookings Institution Press, p. 163; Daniel Kurtzer et al., *The Peace Puzzle*, p. 150.
15 The Israeli Information Center for Human Rights in the Occupied Territories. *Fatalities in the Occupied Territories and Israel*. Available at https://statistics.btselem.org/en/intro/fatalities
16 Avi Shlaim, *The Iron Wall*, p. 713.
17 Avi Shlaim, *The Iron Wall*, p. 713.
18 Amnesty International. 2002. *Israel and the Occupied Territories. Shielded from scrutiny: IDF Violations in Jenin and Nablus* (November). Available at www.amnesty.org/en/wp-content/uploads/2021/10/mde151432002en.pdf
19 Avi Shlaim, *The Iron Wall*, pp. 762–765.
20 Avi Shlaim, *The Iron Wall*, p. 762.
21 Avi Shlaim, *The Iron Wall*, p. 752.
22 Hirsch-Hoefler and Mudde, *The Israeli Settler Movement*, p. 51.

23 The Israel Information Center for Human Rights in the Occupied Territories. 2006. *683 People Killed in the Conflict in 2006* (December 28). Available at www.btselem.org/press_releases/20061228
24 Ian Black. 2017. *Enemies and Neighbors: Arabs and Jews in Palestine and Israel, 1917–2017*. New York: Atlantic Monthly Press, p. 416; Human Rights Watch. 2007. *Why They Died* (September 5). Available at www.hrw.org/report/2007/09/05/why-they-died/civilian-casualties-lebanon-during-2006-war
25 Daniel Kurtzer et al., *The Peace Puzzle*, p. 219.
26 The Naval Vessel Transfer Act (Public Law 110–429) is available at www.govinfo.gov/content/pkg/PLAW-110publ429/html/PLAW-110publ429.htm
27 Ian Black, *Enemies and Neighbors*, p. 424.
28 Norman Finkelstein. 2018. *Gaza: An Inquest into Its Martyrdom*. Oakland, CA: California University Press, pp. 14–15.
29 The Israeli Information Center for Human Rights in the Occupied Territories. *Fatalities in the Occupied Territories and Israel*. Available at https://statistics.btselem.org/en/intro/fatalities
30 Obama's speech is available at https://obamawhitehouse.archives.gov/issues/foreign-policy/presidents-speech-cairo-a-new-beginning
31 Khaled Elgindy, *The Blind Spot*, p. 209.
32 The Israeli Information Center for Human Rights in the Occupied Territories. 2013. *Human Rights Violations during Operation Pillar of Defense* (May 13). Available at www.btselem.org/download/201305_pillar_of_defense_operation_eng.pdf
33 The Israeli Information Center for Human Rights in the Occupied Territories. 2016. *50 Days: More Than 500 Children: Facts and Figures on Fatalities in Gaza, Summer 2014* (July 20). Available at www.btselem.org/press_releases/20160720_fatalities_in_gaza_conflict_2014
34 Max Fisher. 2014. *This Chart Shows Every Person Killed in the Israel-Palestine Conflict Since 2000* (July 14). Available at www.vox.com/2014/7/14/5898581/chart-israel-palestine-conflict-deaths

7 Into the Present

It is fair to say that almost all, if not all, U.S. presidents have been more sympathetic to Israel than to Palestinians, often significantly more. When Donald Trump assumed the presidency in 2017, he quickly proved to be the most aggressive pro-Israel president to date. During his presidential campaign, he realized quickly that his fortunes would be increased by relying on a Christian evangelical base and Zionist organizations. In March 2016, he told the American Israel Public Affairs Committee (AIPAC) audience, "We will send a clear signal that there is no daylight between America and our most reliable ally, the State of Israel." Regarding the Palestinians, he said that they "must come to the table knowing that the bond between the United States and Israel is absolutely, totally unbreakable." And then, as he contended for a second term, Trump announced, "The Jewish state has never had a better friend in the White House than your president, Donald J. Trump."

In contrast to Donald Trump, Joe Biden has a long political history reaching back to the early 1970s when he was elected U.S. Senator for Delaware. In 1973, just shortly after the October War, he met with the Israeli Prime Minister Golda Meir, a meeting he later described as "one of the most consequential" of his life. More recently, after he became Barack Obama's running mate in the 2008 presidential elections, he declared himself to be a Zionist. In 2021, he became president himself, and in July 2022, he took his presidential maiden trip to the Middle East. It would be his tenth time in Israel. Upon arrival at the airport, he promised strong support for Israel's military, stating, "The connection between the Israeli people and the American people is bone deep. It's bone deep." In late 2023, subsequently, he demonstrated unconditional support for Israel, even as the latter was unleashing an unprecedented bombing campaign on Gaza.

DOI: 10.4324/9781003536260-7

Descent into Apartheid

Just a few weeks before Donald Trump announced his presidential candidacy in June 2015, Benjamin Netanyahu had won a third consecutive term as prime minister. He formed what was widely hailed as the most right-wing government in the country's history. More than half of his new cabinet, himself included, opposed the establishment of a sovereign Palestinian state. Amid continued Israeli settlement projects on Palestinian lands, the outgoing Obama administration had already been compelled to concede that prospects for a Palestinian state looked grim, warning that Israel could become an apartheid state. Just a few years earlier, in 2012, the UN Committee on the Elimination of All Forms of Racial Discrimination reached the same conclusion, stating that the "hermetic character of the separation of two groups" in the Occupied Territories is akin to apartheid.[1]

What is apartheid? Historically, the term is associated with South Africa. There, it described a system of political, economic, and social domination by an all-white government over the non-white majority that lasted until 1994. In 2002, as the International Criminal Court (ICC) was established, the crime of apartheid was disassociated from its South African origin. Henceforth, it could be applied anywhere in the world. According to the Rome Statute, which is the ICC's founding document, apartheid consists of "inhumane acts ... committed in the context of an institutionalized regime of systematic oppression and domination by one racial group over any other racial group or groups ...." These acts include "deportation or forcible transfer of population" and "persecution against any identifiable group or collectivity on political, racial, national, ethnic, cultural, religious, gender ... or other [inadmissible] grounds."[2]

After Israel had been occupying Palestinian lands for decades, charges of apartheid have become more common. For much of the 2000s, the UN Special Rapporteur on the Situation of Human Rights in the Palestinian Occupied Territories was John Dugard, incidentally a South African lawyer. In his 2007 report, he wrote, "elements of the Israeli occupation constitute forms of colonialism and of apartheid ...."[3] Dugard's successor was the Jewish-American Princeton law professor Richard Falk. In his 2014 report he wrote, "Through prolonged occupation, with practices and policies which appear to constitute apartheid and segregation, ongoing expansion of settlements, and continual construction of the wall arguably amounting to de facto annexation of parts of the occupied Palestinian territory, the denial by Israel of the right to self-determination of the Palestinian people is evident."[4]

Expectedly, such charges are routinely and squarely rejected by leading Israeli politicians as well as other governments, perhaps most prominently those of the U.S., Germany, and France. Allegations of apartheid against Israel are also often referred to as blatantly absurd, biased, or even Anti-semitic. Over the years, however, charges would become more and more frequent and substantiated and, in fact, they would evolve into a consensus of the world's most authoritative human rights organizations.

In 2021, Human Rights Watch wrote, "[Israeli] authorities have dispossessed, confined, forcibly separated, and subjugated Palestinians by virtue of their identity to varying degrees of intensity. In certain areas, ..., these deprivations are so severe that they amount to the crimes against humanity of apartheid and persecution."[5] Amnesty International, another leading global human rights organization, concluded that Israel's "institutionalized regime of oppression and domination" must be "defined as apartheid under international law."[6] The Israeli human rights organization B'Tselem reached a very similar conclusion, writing, "The Israeli regime enacts in all the territory it controls (Israeli sovereign territory, East Jerusalem, the West Bank, and the Gaza Strip) an apartheid regime."[7]

In 2022 alone, two successive UN Special Rapporteurs made similar allegations. In his report, Michael Lynk concluded that the "political system of entrenched rule in the Occupied Palestinian Territory that endows one racial-national-ethnic group with substantial rights, benefits and privileges while intentionally subjecting another group to live behind walls and checkpoints and under a permanent military rule" without rights, equality, dignity, and freedom "satisfies the prevailing evidentiary standard for the existence of apartheid."[8] Shortly afterwards, Lynk's successor, Francesca Albanese, called for the UN General Assembly to develop "a plan to end the Israeli settler-colonial occupation and apartheid regime."[9]

The Trump Presidency

The Obama administration knew that Israel was progressing toward being an apartheid regime, but it continued to defend Israel nevertheless. In September 2016, it approved a ten-year, $38 billion military aid package, the largest U.S. pledge to Israel ever. These funds were offered without concrete policy demands regarding Palestinian rights or statehood. Despite the Obama administration's unprecedented monetary support for Israel, Donald Trump lambasted his predecessor as the worst thing that happened to Israel.

The new president would break new ground, in a literal sense. Barely one year into his administration, on December 6, 2017, Trump announced the U.S.'s recognition of Jerusalem as Israel's undivided capital and the U.S. plan to move its embassy from Tel Aviv to Jerusalem. Prime Minister Benjamin Netanyahu hailed December 6 as a "historic day." For his part, Palestinian President Mahmoud Abbas announced that the U.S. had disqualified itself from the role as a peace broker and thus severed official ties with the administration. The White House soon retaliated by cutting all its assistance to the UN Relief and Works Agency for Palestine Refugees (UNRWA). Since 1949, the agency has been in charge of providing education, health, and social services to Palestinian refugees.

The Jerusalem decision was a violation of international law. One day after Trump's announcement, the UN Security Council held an emergency meeting. Fourteen out of fifteen members condemned the decision. Expectedly, the U.S. vetoed any further action. On December 21, it was the General Assembly's turn to deliberate the issue. An overwhelming majority of 128 states rejected the recognition of Jerusalem as Israel's capital. Legally, however, the vote of the General Assembly was not binding and thus it made no difference on the ground. On May 14, 2018, the new embassy was officially opened. Not long after, the Trump administration also declared that it did not see the illegal Jewish settlements in the West Bank as a hindrance to peace, and in March 2019, it recognized Israeli sovereignty over the Syrian Golan Heights.

The new U.S. embassy in Jerusalem opened its doors on the 70th anniversary of Israel's founding, but this was also the eve of the Palestinian al-Nakba Day. A few weeks earlier, tens of thousands of Gazans had started rallying every Friday near the border fence in what they dubbed the Great March of Return. As the name suggests, Gazans demanded the right to return to their familial homes they were forced to leave decades before. With most Gazans being refugees, they had been living under a blockade since 2007 and under occupation for more than fifty years.

Although the rallies were largely non-violent, some protesters threw stones or Molotov cocktails or flew kites and balloons with burning rags across the fence. The IDF, once again, responded with overwhelming force, namely with tanks, rubber bullets, live ammunition, and tear gas. On the eve of the Nakba's anniversary alone, Israeli forces killed about sixty Palestinians who did not pose a direct threat.[10] At the same time, members of the Trump family, along with Republican leaders, were celebrating in Jerusalem. The protests lasted through 2019, and by the end, more than 220 Palestinians were killed, forty-six of them minors. Some 8,000 were injured, many of them shot in the lower limbs so as to maim them.[11]

Palestinians were forcefully subdued and ever more marginalized, both politically and legally. In July, the Knesset passed the Nation State Law, proclaiming Israel as "the nation-state of the Jewish people." According to the law, "the right to exercise national self-determination in the State of Israel is unique to the Jewish people." The law also declares "a greater, united Jerusalem" to be the capital of Israel, thus reaffirming the illegal annexation of East Jerusalem. It endorses Judaization – the development of Jewish-only settlements. While the Israeli leadership reasoned the law by referencing sovereign rights, international observers and human rights advocates have emphasized that the law, in fact, was institutionalizing Jewish supremacy and therewith elements of apartheid.

The next blow to Palestinians came in January 2020 when Donald Trump presented what he had been referring to as the "deal of the century." It purported to provide for an end to the conflict through a two-state solution. It was quickly obvious, however, that the proposed Palestinian state would not really amount to one. The majority of illegal settlements in the Occupied Territories would become part of Israel, as would the Jordan Valley. Jerusalem would be the country's undivided capital. Palestinians would retain some control of only about 15 percent of historic Palestine. Roads would connect the Palestinian patches of land, and these would be controlled by Israel, as would Palestine's borders and airspace. The internationally recognized right of return for Palestinian refugees would be erased. In return for all these concessions, Palestinians would receive some $50 billion in investment over ten years.

Trump's plan was the product of Israeli interests. Palestinians were not even consulted. It was entirely void of their claims, and the Palestinian leadership rejected it immediately. Palestinian isolation would go yet further with U.S. efforts to reshuffle the geopolitics of the region with the 2020 Abraham Accords. Since 1979, Iran had been a foe not only to the U.S. but also to Israel as well as to several Arab countries. A chief intent of the Accords was to ally these countries against Iran. Toward this end they committed Israel, on the one side, and the United Arab Emirates, Bahrain, Sudan, and Morocco, on the other, to normalize their relations. Historically, these Arab countries had insisted that they would not normalize relations with Israel until there would be a sovereign Palestinian state. The U.S., however, managed to persuade the leadership of these countries into the Accords and, with that, the Palestinian predicament was seriously downgraded.

Into the Present

In 2020, it was not clear whether Trump could secure a second presidential term. Israeli leaders favored him and they planned to name a settlement in the occupied Golan Heights after him – Trump Heights. Trump lost, however, and in January 2021 he was succeeded by Joseph Biden. Although Biden seemed starkly different from Trump, at least in regard to Middle East Policy, there was a lot of continuation. Biden, like Trump, continued to cooperate with Arab autocrats and build on Trump's Abraham Accords. Moreover, although the new administration came in with rhetoric about a Palestinian state, it would not do anything toward its realization. In fact, the administration largely stopped any criticism of Israeli settlement expansion, which had always been seen as the chief barrier for the manifestation of a two-state solution.

Just a few days after Biden was sworn in, the International Criminal Court had declared its jurisdiction over the territories occupied by Israel since 1967, namely Gaza, the West Bank, and East Jerusalem. It would investigate the 2014 Gaza War, Israeli settlement policy in the Occupied Territories as well as the 2018–2019 Gaza border clashes. To be sure, it was not only alleged Israeli crimes that were on the table. Early on, the prosecutor remarked that Hamas and other Palestinian armed groups may be guilty of war crimes as they had indiscriminately targeted Israeli civilians and used Palestinian civilians as human shields. The Palestinian Authority declared its full cooperation. Israel, on the other hand, declared that the court would have no authority.

Benjamin Netanyahu, in the meantime, was facing his own legal issues. In 2019 he had been charged with corruption, and his trial began the following year. Moreover, his government coalition was seriously damaged, coming to a halt in late 2020. However, the new government also proved inherently unstable, and just eighteen months after he lost his premiership, Netanyahu would accede to that position once again. His Likud party formed an alliance with the religious Zionist and ultra-orthodox parties, all of whom were carried by Greater Israel ambitions and were determined to continue with illegal settlements on Palestinian land. The new government was to be sworn in at the end of the year and, once again, it was hailed as the most extreme far-right government in Israel's history around the world.

The Palestinian outlook was grim. In early 2021, the East Jerusalem neighborhood of Sheikh Jarrah had become the focus of international attention. The Israeli Supreme Court threatened long-time Palestinian residents with eviction, while their homes would be transferred to Jewish settlers. Palestinians held protests around East Jerusalem, and on May 7, the Haram al-Sharif/Temple Mount became the site of a major escalation. After thousands of Muslims had attended Friday prayers, there were skirmishes between some attendees and Israeli police. Protesters threw rocks and police responded with overwhelming force, including stun grenades, rubber bullets, and tear gas. A few days later, police stormed the compound again and the escalation spread across the city and the West Bank.

In Gaza, Hamas posed an ultimatum for Israel to withdraw its forces both from the Sheikh Jarrah neighborhood and the Haram al-Sharif. When it was ignored, Hamas fired rockets toward Israeli towns. Israel responded with missiles and artillery strikes over the land strip. The fighting lasted for eleven days during which the U.S. repeatedly blocked a UN Security Council statement calling for an end of hostilities. In the period between May 10 and 21, there were nearly 280 casualties across the Occupied Territories. At least 130 of them were civilians, including dozens of children. In Israel, thirteen people were killed, including two children and six women.[12]

About a year later there was another renewed escalation of violence in Gaza, which was again preceded by happenings in the West Bank. Violence by zealous Jewish settlers against Palestinian civilians had been spreading in recent years and became ever more aggressive. Through intimidation these settlers were aiming to take over more and more Palestinian land. Palestinians were attacked in their homes; their property and olive groves were destroyed, and communities were harassed and assaulted. According to the security agreement the Palestinian Authority (PA) held with Israel, Palestinian police were not allowed to restrain Jewish settlers. In the past, the Israeli government had, at times, condemned the acts of these settlers and Israeli security had held them back, but this was happening ever less. In fact, security forces were now seen facilitating the violence.

Parallel to the escalation of settler violence was the formation of new Palestinian resistance groups with names such as the Jenin Brigade or the Nablus Brigade. In defiance of the PA, they were set on fighting the Israeli occupation from hideouts in refugee camps and towns. They engaged in shootouts during Israeli raids as well as shootings of Israeli military checkpoints. In the first month of 2022, some of these brigades were involved in a series of deadly attacks that killed nearly twenty Israelis. Israel responded with Operation Break the Wave, a campaign of almost daily raids on Palestinian homes, resulting in mass arrests and dozens of casualties. Among those arrested was a leader of Islamic Jihad. The campaign would soon extend to Gaza, where the group had its home base. On August 5, Israel launched a wave of air attacks on Gaza, while the Palestinian Islamic Jihad fired hundreds of rockets at Israel. With an Egyptian-mediated truce, the fighting ended after three days.

As the year was coming to an end, it was widely described as the deadliest year in more than one and a half decades. But, as in all previous escalations, the deaths were disproportionally on the Palestinian side. About 180 Palestinians were killed, with a significant number of minors and women. On the Israeli side, there were over twenty casualties, the majority of them civilians, as well as three foreign nationals.[13] It was also at the end of the year that Netanyahu's new government was sworn in. For the occasion, he tweeted, "The Jewish people have an exclusive and unquestionable right to all areas of the Land of Israel." He continued, "The government will promote and develop settlement in all parts of the Land of Israel — in the Galilee, the Negev, the Golan, Judea and Samaria [the occupied West Bank]." As the government was sworn in, the U.S. Ambassador tweeted, "Here's to the rock-solid U.S.-Israel relationship and unbreakable ties."

As the year 2023 progressed, there were signs that it could become even more deadly than the preceding one. Settler violence continued and at the beginning of the year, Israeli forces raided the Jenin refugee camp and killed nine Palestinians. In return, a Palestinian gunman shot dead seven Israelis near a Jerusalem synagogue, the deadliest assault on Israelis in fifteen years. In late February, two Jewish settlers were killed as they drove though the Palestinian town of Huwara. In retaliation, hundreds of settlers descended violently on the town, burning houses and vehicles in a rampage that even former Israeli Prime Minister Ehud Olmert referred to as a pogrom, a term we encountered in the opening chapter to this book. In the first nine months of the year, as Human Rights Watch put it, "Israeli security forces killed more Palestinians in the West Bank – 192, including 40 children – than in any other year since 2005, when the United Nations began systematically recording fatalities."[14]

On October 7, Hamas, spurred by the ongoing occupation, the oppression of apartheid, the expansion of settlements in the West Bank, the blockade on Gaza, infringements upon the Haram al-Sharif, and various other grievances, launched an unprecedented attack on military targets and civilians in southern Israel. About 1,150 were killed and about 250 people were taken hostage. Of those killed, close to 800 were civilians. For Israel, it was the greatest loss of life in a single day since its founding in 1948.[15] The country was in severe shock and was pervaded by an intense mood for vengeance. It responded with what came to be one of the deadliest and most destructive bombing campaigns in modern international history. The rather primitive rockets that Hamas continued to fire at times did not pose any real danger to Israel.

A few days after Israel's first air strikes, the IDF ordered 1.1 million Palestinians in the northern half of the Strip to abandon their homes and trek south. In the first week alone, the Israeli Air Force dropped around 1,000 bombs a day.[16] As the assault continued, the supposedly safer zone in the south was not spared. At the end of October, the IDF launched a massive ground invasion into northern Gaza and it soon expanded into the south. Evacuation orders were now also issued here, gradually pushing hundreds of thousands into the most southern city of Rafah, on Gaza's border with Egypt. On December 5, a UN official declared, "Nowhere is safe in Gaza. Not hospitals, not shelters, not refugee camps. No one is safe. Not children. Not health workers. Not humanitarians."[17] Israel justified its indiscriminate bombing by stating that Hamas was hiding in schools and hospitals and using civilians as human shields.

By mid-March, five months into the wear, the death toll in Gaza has reached more than 31,000. The vast majority of the casualties are unrelated to Hamas. Of the dead, at least 9,000 are women and 13,000 are children. Adults and children alike are suffering catastrophic injuries and these will leave once again another generation of maimed Palestinians. More than 65,000 housing units have been destroyed. Hospitals, schools, universities, grocery stores, mosques, and churches have also been damaged or destroyed, and nearly all of Gaza's population is displaced. It should also be noted here that more than 120 reporters and media workers have been killed, as well as over 165 UN staff members, the highest number of aid workers killed in any conflict in the organization's history.[18] Since the beginning of Israel's ground offensive, 249 soldiers have died.[19] Dozens of hostages have also been killed.

From the beginning of its military campaign, Israel has also intensified its long-running siege of Gaza into a "complete siege," exacerbating the already existing humanitarian crisis. Thus, this led to a serious shortage of all life essentials – electricity, food, water, medical supplies, and medicine. Early on, various humanitarian and relief organizations warned of spreading diseases and famine in Gaza. In fact, Israel was soon charged with using starvation of civilians as a weapon of war in Gaza.[20] It was also early on that human rights activists and scholars referred to the Israeli bombardment and its siege as a genocide. The 1948 United Nations Convention on the Prevention and Punishment of the Crime of Genocide defines genocide as "acts committed with intent to destroy, in whole or in part, a national, ethnical, racial or religious group, as such."

At the end of 2023, South Africa had taken the initiative and filed this charge of genocide against Israel at the International Court of Justice (ICJ) in Den Haag. After several days of hearings in January, the Court judged that indeed Israel's conduct could plausibly constitute genocide. It issued several provisional orders to Israel, including that it must take measures to prevent genocide, ensure that its military does not commit genocide, take measures to prevent and punish incitement to genocide, and take immediate measures to enable urgent humanitarian assistance and basic services. A final verdict on whether Israel is guilty of genocide is pending. But regardless of the court's final judgement, what Israel has inflicted upon Gaza, the daily increasing death toll and the nearly total destruction of Gaza, is indeed catastrophic.

It should be noted that this latest war on Gaza, once again, has implications for wider international politics. We saw above that Israel and various Arab leaders have been intent on normalizing relations with each other. The unfolding catastrophe and popular sympathies for the Palestinian people across the Arab world complicate these ambitions. In light of the region's popular sympathies for Palestinians, these Arab leaders are becoming even more illegitimate in their people's eyes than they were all along. Then there is, of course, also the danger of a wider regional escalation. Lebanon's Hezbollah is in solidarity with Hamas and so there are periodic clashes with Israel. At the same time, the Yemeni Houthi movement is attacking commercial ships in the Red Sea they say are linked to Israel. It declared its commitment to continue these until Israel ends its military campaign.

Hamas, Hezbollah, the Houthis, together with the Palestinian Islamic Jihad, Iran, and further groups in Iraq and Syria constitute the so-called axis of resistance. This alliance came into being in the aftermath of the U.S. 2003 invasion of Iraq and was given new life with the October 7 attacks. What binds this group is a shared hatred of U.S. meddling in the region and its support of Israel. Although each of the members have their own local interest, together they are also committed to the Palestinian cause. Although the alliance is militarily no match to the IDF, their collective commitment and their multiple fronts is very troubling to Israel. The U.S. has not remained unaffected either. Regarding the Houthis, for example, it has led a number of countries in retaliatory strikes.

This leads to the last point of this chapter. Insofar as the international community has been engaging in efforts to halt the unfolding catastrophe, these were regularly obstructed by the U.S. In the UN Security Council, for example, the U.S. vetoed three attempts at a ceasefire. From the beginning the Biden administration has also lent unconditional support to Israel in the realm of providing weapons and munitions and even as the charge of genocide was initiated against Israel, this supply continued.

Conclusion

Since the 1990s, Israeli politics has been characterized by a steady rightward shift and a descent into open apartheid. Arguably the situation in Israel and the Occupied Palestinian Territories was never as bad as it is today. While Western leaders have agreed that Hamas must be held accountable for its October 7, 2023 attack, for Israel, such an insistence has remained largely absent. Throughout the period reviewed in this chapter, American leaders stood by Israel. Without any accountability, we are once again reminded of Thucydides' dictum that the strong do what they have the power to do, even when this may constitute a case of genocide.

The weak, for their part, continue to resist, but as Palestinians are losing more and more of their land, they are also incurring countless casualties, affecting every family. The innumerable condemnations of Israel's doings by many human rights organizations are a testimony to the injustice that has continued to unfold for many decades. There is little doubt that a regime of apartheid will be unable to sustain itself in the long term; yet, in the short term the extent of the suffering will depend on the U.S. and whether its relationship with Israel remains unconditional, allowing power politics to reign supreme while marginalizing politics of justice.

Suggested Further Readings

Erakat, Noura. 2019. *Justice for Some: Law and the Question of Palestine*. Stanford, CA: Stanford University Press.

Falk, Richard, John Dugard, and Michael Lynk. 2023. *Protecting Human Rights in Occupied Palestine: Working Through the United Nations*. Atlanta, GA: Clarity Press.

Slater, Jerome. 2020. *Mythologies Without End: The US, Israel, and the Arab-Israeli Conflict, 1917–2020*. New York: Oxford University Press.

Notes

1 Committee on the Elimination of Racial Discrimination. 2012. *Consideration of Reports Submitted by States Parties under Article 9 of the Convention* (March 9, advance unedited version). Available at www2.ohchr.org/english/bodies/cerd/docs/cerd.c.isr.co.14-16.pdf

2 The International Criminal Court. 2011. *The Rome Statute of the International Criminal Court*. Available at www.icc-cpi.int/sites/default/files/RS-Eng.pdf

3 John Dugard. 2007. *Report of the Special Rapporteur on the Situation of Human Rights in the Palestinian Territories Occupied Since 1967* (January 29). Available at https://digitallibrary.un.org/record/593075?ln=en&v=pdf

4 Richard Falk. 2014. *Report of the Special Rapporteur on the Situation of Human Rights in the Palestinian Territories Occupied Since 1967* (January 13). Available at www.ohchr.org/sites/default/files/HRBodies/HRC/RegularSessions/Session25/Documents/A-HRC-25-67_en.doc

5 Human Rights Watch. 2021. *A Threshold Crossed: Israeli Authorities and the Crimes of Apartheid and Persecution*. www.hrw.org/report/2021/04/27/threshold-crossed/israeli-authorities-and-crimes-apartheid-and-persecution

6 Amnesty International. 2022. *Israel's Apartheid Against Palestinians: A Cruel System of Domination and a Crime Against Humanity*. Available at www.

amnesty.org/en/latest/news/2022/02/israels-apartheid-against-palestinians-a-cruel-system-of-domination-and-a-crime-against-humanity/

7 The Israeli Information Center for Human Rights in the Occupied Territories. 2021. *A Regime of Jewish Supremacy from the Jordan River to the Mediterranean Sea: This is Apartheid*. Available at www.btselem.org/apartheid

8 Michael Lynk. 2022. *Report of the Special Rapporteur on the Situation of Human Rights in the Palestinian Territories Occupied Since 1967* (March 22, advance unedited version). Available at www.un.org/unispal/wp-content/uploads/2022/03/A_HRC_49_87_210321.pdf

9 Francesca Albanese. 2022. *Situation of Human Rights in the Palestinian Territories Occupied since 1967* (September 21). Available at www.un.org/unispal/wp-content/uploads/2022/10/A.77.356_210922.pdf

10 Amnesty International. 2018. *Six Months On: Gaza's Great March of Return* (October 19). Available at www.amnesty.org/en/latest/campaigns/2018/10/gaza-great-march-of-return/

11 The Israeli Information Center for Human Rights in the Occupied Territories. 2021. *Unwilling and Unable: Israel's Whitewashed Investigations of the Great March of Return* (December). Available at www.btselem.org/sites/default/files/publications/202112_unwilling_and_unable_eng.pdf

12 United Nations Office for the Coordination of Humanitarian Affairs. 2021. *Protection of Civilians Report; 24–31 May 2021* (June 4). Available at www.ochaopt.org/poc/24-31-may-2021

13 The Israeli Information Center for Human Rights in the Occupied Territories. 2023. *The Occupied Territories in 2022: Largest Number of Palestinians Killed by Israel in the West Bank Since 2004* (January 8). Available at www.btselem.org/press_releases/20230108_the_occupied_territories_in_2022_largest_number_of_palestinians_killed_by_israel_in_the_west_bank_since_2004

14 Omar Shakir. 2023. *While a Fire Rages in Gaza, the West Bank Smolders*. Human Rights Watch (November 22). Available at www.hrw.org/news/2023/11/22/while-fire-rages-gaza-west-bank-smolders

15 Eado Hecht. 2024. *The Gaza Terror Offensive*. The Begin-Sadat Center for Strategic Studies at Bar-Ilan University. Available at https://besacenter.org/the-gaza-terror-offensive-october-7-8-2023/; Agence France Press. 2023. *Israel Social Security Data Reveals True Picture of Oct 7 Deaths* (December 15). Available at www.france24.com/en/live-news/20231215-israel-social-security-data-reveals-true-picture-of-oct-7-deaths

16 Information from X site of the Israeli Air Force. Available at https://twitter.com/IAFsite/status/1712484101763342772?lang=en

17 The UN Office for the Coordination of Humanitarian Affairs in the Occupied Palestinian Territory. December 6, 2023. Available at https://twitter.com/ochaopt/status/1732205763831943611

18 The UN Office for the Coordination of Humanitarian Affairs in the Occupied Palestinian Territory. 2024. *Hostilities in the Gaza Strip and Israel - Reported Impact | Day 157* (March 12). Available at www.ochaopt.org/content/hostilities-gaza-strip-and-israel-reported-impact-day-157

19 Israeli Ministry of Foreign Affairs. *2024. Swords of Iron: IDF Casualties*. Available at www.gov.il/en/departments/news/swords-of-iron-idf-casualties#

20 Huma Rights Watch. 2023. *Israel: Starvation Used as Weapon of War in Gaza*, (December 18). Available at www.hrw.org/news/2023/12/18/israel-starvation-used-weapon-war-gaza#

8 Toward What Outcome?

We began this book with the historian Thucydides and his account of the Melian Dialogue from the year 416 BCE. The Melians and the Athenians were disputing over the future of Melos. The Melians were weak and the Athenians were strong. In the course of the exchange, the Athenians justified their intention to colonize the island of Melos, explaining that "it is a general and necessary law of nature to rule whatever one can." They continued by urging their Melian counterparts to submit to this edict:

> You will see that there is nothing disgraceful in giving way to the greatest city in Hellas when she is offering you such reasonable terms ... And when you are allowed to choose between war and safety, you will not be so insensitively arrogant as to make the wrong choice. This is the safe rule – to stand up to one's equals, to behave with deference to one's superiors, and to treat one's inferiors with moderation.[1]

The conflict between Melos and Athens continues to highlight the most important aspect in international politics, including the Israeli-Palestinian conflict, namely the preeminence of power. It is indeed as Thucydides recorded the Athenians saying, "The strong do what they have the power to do and the weak accept what they have to accept." For over a hundred years, the Israelis have been the stronger party in the conflict. Beginning with the First World War, the Yishuv had the support of the British Empire. Beginning in the 1940s, the Zionist movement could increasingly count on American support and since the 1967 War, the latter's military and political support became increasingly unconditional. As a result, the majority of what was once Palestine became Israel. Other large swaths of Palestine became occupied and colonized, a development that continues to the present day.

DOI: 10.4324/9781003536260-8

Matters of fairness and justice were irrelevant in the conflict between Athens and Melos. It was deference that the Athenians were expecting from the Melians, and they stated that such conduct would be the wise choice for the Melians. Matters of fairness and justice have proven equally futile, if not irrelevant, in the Israeli-Palestinian conflict as the international community has failed to hold Israel to the standards and requirements of international law. In fact, the U.S., Israel's chief ally, has gone so far as to label legal challenges against Israel as illegitimate warfare, or "lawfare."[2] However, just as the Melians would not engage in the deference demanded by Athenians, Palestinians have not shown deference.

As we have seen throughout this book, Palestinians have engaged in acts of resistance, including illegal resistance, resulting in many innocent Israeli casualties. In a relative perspective, however, it is evident that Palestinian violence is not comparable to Israeli violence. As we have seen in Chapter 6, for example, the number of Palestinians killed in the conflict is incomparably higher that the number of Israelis killed. In more recent years, this statistic has become even more lopsided. It is a regrettable exercise to compare casualty numbers, but, at the same time, they are manifest evidence for the conclusion that what has been done to Palestinians is wholly on a different scale than what has been done to Israelis.

Where might the history that we explored in this book be leading to? In the remainder of this final chapter, we shall discuss this question. In the literature on the Israeli-Palestinian conflict, there is often a discussion of two possible outcomes (sometimes referred to as two solutions). Let's start by laying out these two outcomes and, in doing so, we shall see the consequences for both Israelis and Palestinians. The chapter will conclude with some critical points about the U.S.'s role in the conflict.

The Two-State Outcome

Historically, the two-state outcome is the one that has been most discussed. As the name suggests, this outcome entails a sovereign Palestinian state alongside a sovereign Jewish state. One of the early proposals toward two states was put forth in the 1937 Peel Plan, as discussed in Chapter 3. In 1947, UN Resolution 148 also envisioned two states, but only one came to be – Israel. The UN's Security Council Resolution 242 from 1967 reemphasized the two-state outcome. In 1988, the Palestinian Liberation Organization (PLO) conceded to such an outcome. The Palestinian state would be limited to the West Bank, Gaza, and East Jerusalem, barely over 20 percent of what once constituted Palestine. It was an enormous concession, and the international consensus thus became that the region's most protracted conflict should be solved in this way.

The fundamentals for such an outcome seemed clear: The Palestinian state would be constituted along the Green Line, that is, the border before the 1967 War. While Palestinians would allow some bigger Jewish settlements located east of the border to become part of Israel, the latter would swap equal territory to Palestinians. Jerusalem would be the shared capital of both Israel and Palestine. While Israel would retain sovereignty over West Jerusalem, Palestinians would gain sovereignty over East Jerusalem. Both sides would be given unhindered access to their respective holy sites, with Israelis retaining sovereignty over the Western Wall and Palestinians over the Haram al-Sharif. Moreover, Israel would acknowledge the unjust displacement of Palestinians, but only a symbolic number of Palestinians would be allowed to return so that Israel's Jewish identity would not be undermined. Other Palestinian refugees would be financially compensated for their loss.

However, as one is reading through the history of the Israeli-Palestinian conflict, it becomes evident that what sounds straightforward on paper has proven very elusive in practice. Historically, it seems that Israel was not willing to allow for a fully sovereign Palestinian state. A critical look at the Oslo process of the 1990s, for example, reveals that while a two-state solution was propagated, Israel was, in fact, making it increasingly impossible, largely due to its ongoing settlement constructions in the West Bank. In recent years, a variety of Israeli leaders have been declaring publicly that they will not allow a sovereign Palestinian state to emerge. What they have been proposing instead is some autonomy in restricted Palestinian areas. Such an outcome is, of course, unacceptable to Palestinians. This poses the following question: In the hypothetical case that the international community, in particular the U.S., would compel Israel to revise its stance, would a two-state outcome still be practicable?

A growing majority of observers are highly critical, saying that Israel has just gone too far with its settlement projects in the West Bank and East Jerusalem. Over the decades Israel has engaged in ongoing campaigns to Judaize Palestinian territories; it has created too many facts on the ground, as it is often said. When the Oslo process started in the early 1990s, there were about 130,000 settlers living in the Occupied Territories. Today, however, there are well over half a million settlers living in these territories, in over 200 settlements. These are connected to each other and to Israel through roads that crisscross through Palestinian lands. The West Bank, in effect, is split into more than twenty separate and small areas, thus making a contiguous Palestinian state impossible.

The One-State Outcome

Given that a two-state outcome has become highly questionable, if not flat out impossible, it is not surprising that the focus has shifted to the idea of a one-state outcome. This idea, in fact, pre-dates the two-state idea, going back at least to the 1920 Brit Shalom (Peace Alliance), an association of Jewish intellectuals. Influenced by personalities like Ahad Ha'am, whom we encountered in Chapter 2, Brit Shalom rejected Zionist ambitions of a Jewish state in Palestine. Instead, they argued for peaceful integration through cultural paths and that Palestine would be a home for two nations. A similar suggestion, as we have seen in Chapter 5, was made by the PLO in the late 1960s.

The advocates of a one-state outcome often contend that it is, in fact, only such a solution that can, with some degree of justice, address the fundamental issues that have fueled the conflict, namely land, Jerusalem, refugees, and settlements. The most straightforward vision here is that a single democratic and secular state would emerge and replace what today is Israel and the Occupied Palestinian Territories. Every citizen, regardless of whether they are Jewish or Palestinian, would have equal rights in every regard. They could also live anywhere they choose. The government would include Jews and Palestinians, and it would be located in Jerusalem.

An alternative scenario would be a binational state. It would be based on the explicit recognition that two national groups live as neighbors in the same country. In this vision, Jews and Palestinians would share political sovereignty while remaining autonomous in managing their communal affairs, in matters of language, education, and culture, for example. Matters of common concern, such as foreign policy and economic policy, would be in the purview of common institutions. One advantage of the binational state is that Zionism could be maintained in some form; the new country could still be a national home for the Jewish people, but it would, of course, cease to be a solely Jewish state.

What are the prospects for a one-state solution, in either variant described here? It is safe to say that, on the Jewish side, it would not come about voluntarily, at least not in the short term. A very significant majority of Jews would reject shared ownership of a land they consider to be all theirs. On the Palestinian side, in contrast, there is growing support. Many Palestinians have given up on the thought that Israel would ever allow a Palestinian state as its neighbor. For them, the idea of statehood has been trumped by a prospect of equal rights and the attainment of a more dignified life.

What must also be mentioned here are serious doubts about whether Jews and Palestinians, after decades of intense hostilities, could live in a common state. On the other hand, there are examples where reconciliation proved possible, such as in Rwanda. The country's Hutus and Tutsis had lived in an antagonistic relationship for decades, and in 1994, it culminated in the massive genocide of about 800,000 Tutsis and moderate Hutus. Today, after many years of deliberative reconciliation processes, the country continues to feel the aftermath of the genocide, but it has also moved forward in a productive way. Observers have also drawn comparisons with the hostilities between the Flemish and the Walloon in Belgium and Protestants and Catholics in Northern Ireland.

To be sure, embarking upon a process of reconciliation toward a democratic one-state outcome would be a very arduous path without any guarantee of success. The continuation of the status quo, however, is nearly guaranteed to lead to more conflict and horrific outcomes for both sides. This leads us to the next point. Usually when people talk about the one-state outcome, they refer to a state in which both Palestinians and Jews have equal rights. However, other scenarios are thinkable as well, namely the apartheid scenario and the expulsion scenario. We have touched on these terms several times earlier in the book. Each one warrants a brief discussion.

The Apartheid Scenario. Since the 1967 War and Israel's subsequent refusal to relinquish the Occupied Territories, scholars, journalists, and politicians have made the argument that Israel might be evolving into an apartheid state. The reason is simple: Israel is controlling ever larger areas of Palestinian lands, yet it is not giving fundamental rights to the Palestinians living on these lands. Prominent American politicians to make the apartheid argument include former Presidents Jimmy Carter and Barack Obama. The latter stated in 2013, "Given the demographics west of the Jordan River, the only way for Israel to endure and thrive as a Jewish and democratic state is through the realization of an independent and viable Palestine."[3] In the absence of a two-state solution, so the implication goes, Israel would become an apartheid state.

Insinuations of apartheid often face immediate backlash and harsh criticism from pro-Israel advocates. In fact, however, leading Israeli politicians have drawn the same grim conclusion. In 2010, Defense Minister and former Prime Minister Ehud Barak declared, "It must be understood that if between the Jordan [River] and the [Mediterranean] Sea there is only one political entity called 'Israel', it will by necessity either be not Jewish or not democratic. If this bloc of millions of Palestinians cannot vote, that will be an apartheid state and we will turn into an apartheid state."[4] A few years prior, in 2007, Prime Minister Ehud

Olmert declared that if the two-state solution collapsed, Israel will "face a South African-style struggle for equal voting rights" and "as soon as that happens, the state of Israel is finished."[5]

Although there are significant differences between the situations in South Africa and Israel, this comparison is, in fact, often made. Commenting on the map of the West Bank, the Israeli politician, writer, and peace activist Uri Avnery wrote, "[It] is very reminiscent of the map of apartheid South Africa. There, the racist government had set up several black 'homelands,' nicknamed Bantustans," each "completely surrounded by the territory of the racist state, cut off from the rest of the world."[6] In 2015, the aforementioned South African UN Rapporteur John Dugard observed, "I have no hesitation in saying that Israel's crimes are infinitely worse than those committed by the apartheid regime of South Africa."

Rather recently, in June 2022, two former Israeli ambassadors to South Africa, Ilan Baruch and Alon Liel, said, "It is time for the world to recognize that what we saw in South Africa decades ago is happening in the occupied Palestinian territories too."[7] And in the summer of 2023, the former Mossad (Israel's equivalent to the American CIA) chief Tamir Pardo stated, "In a territory where two people are judged under two legal systems, that is an apartheid state."[8] Finally, as we have seen in the preceding chapter, conclusions of Israeli apartheid are not limited to individuals. The world's leading human rights organizations have issued the same judgement.

The Expulsion Scenario. It is also thinkable that Israel would, on a large scale, expel Palestinians from the Occupied Territories. Palestinians would be either (coercively) incentivized or just bluntly forced to leave their homes, most of them settling in one of the neighboring Arab countries. This strategy has rarely been discussed openly, probably because of its abhorrent nature, but it has a long-standing history. Indeed, its history started with the inception of political Zionism. As illustrated in Chapter 2, in 1885, Theodor Herzl wrote in his diary that it may well be necessary to "expropriate gently the private property on the state assigned to us" and "spirit the penniless population across the border by procuring employment for it in the transit countries, while denying it employment in our country."

Amid the Arab Revolt of the late 1930s and the subsequent Holocaust in Germany, the idea of expulsion became more acute among the Zionist leadership. In 1938, Ben-Gurion acknowledged that "with compulsory transfer we [would] have a vast area [for settlement] … I support compulsory transfer. I don't see anything immoral in it."[9] Other Zionist leaders at the time and afterwards agreed. In 1947 and 1948, Israel did indeed engage in the ethnic cleansing of Palestine and masses of

Palestinians were forced to flee, never allowed to return. Also, in the 1967 War and its aftermath, many Palestinians were expelled from their homelands and were barred from ever returning.[10]

Today, Palestinians are afraid that they may be expelled again. With Israeli politics moving ever further to the right, issues of annexation and population transfers have become rather normalized concepts within Israeli mainstream discussions. An example came to global attention in 2021 when Jewish settlers were forcing the evictions of long-time residents in the East Jerusalem neighborhood of Sheikh Jarrah, as mentioned in Chapter 7. Sheikh Jarrah, however, is only one example of what is happening to Palestinian neighborhoods in Jerusalem and in the West Bank where court-ordered evictions, house demolitions, and displacements have become common occurrences.

In late 2023, things got yet worse. Hamas' attacks on October 7 led to an unprecedented Israeli assault on Gaza. At the moment of this writing, more than 31,000 Gazans have been killed. As the attacks unfolded, international observers ever more often used the term ethnic cleansing to describe Israeli intentions and soon the charge of genocide was also invoked. While the final verdict from the International Court of Justice is pending, an increasing number of scholars and experts agree with the charge. Meanwhile, it is already clear now that the destruction Israel has wrought upon Gaza has made it uninhabitable.

That Israel is labeled an apartheid state and that it is resorting to means of expulsion and arguably genocide is a tragic conclusion. Historically, as we have reviewed in Chapter 2, Jews have a history of being persecuted. In Europe, they faced centuries of oppression, culminating in brutal pogroms and the Holocaust. However, once they accomplished having their own state and were in the possession of "Jewish power," as the Jewish writer Peter Beinart labels it, they evolved from being a victim to being a victimizer. In his book *The Crisis of Zionism*, Beinart writes, "[a]s painful as it is for Jews to admit that race hatred can take root among a people that has suffered so profoundly from it, the ground truth is this: Occupying another people requires racism, and breeds it."[11]

The Role of the United States

Amid the discussion of different outcomes, whether hopeful or abhorrent, there is one current reality and it presents itself as follows: In the area that was once Mandatory Palestine, there is only one state today, Israel, and it rules all Israelis and all Palestinians. In Israel proper, Palestinians are treated as second-class citizens. In the Occupied Territories, Israel denies citizenship to Palestinians, but, at the same time, controls fundamental parts of their lives. It controls who's allowed to enter or exit, who can travel where, who can build or own a house, who's house is to be demolished, and who will be dispossessed. For decades, Israel has kept Palestinians subject to military rule while allowing, or even encouraging, hundreds of thousands of its own citizens to settle on taken land.

The U.S. has been complicit in these developments. Since the onset of the Cold War, the U.S. has been a significant player in the Middle East. Throughout the Cold War, its goal was to protect access to oil and to deter a communist advance. With Israel's spectacular victory in the 1967 War, it proved its military prowess and that it would be a strategic asset to the U. S., first in Cold War issues but then also beyond. In the meantime, its strategic value has become very dubious, but Washington leaders have held on to their initial beliefs. Thus, they have consistently protected Israel from any real accountability, for example, by using its Security Council veto on behalf of Israel dozens of times over the decades.

Strategic reasons for the U.S.'s support of Israel were always complemented by ideological factors and by domestic politics. In fact, this was already the case for President Truman in the 1940s. Zionist lobbying held much sway in Washington and, over time, this influence became very organized through the American Israel Public Affairs Committee (AIPAC). Through its considerable resources, AIPAC has been able to shape public opinion as well as influence U.S. legislators and key decision makers. Because of AIPAC's work, as long-time Israeli Prime Minister Benjamin Netanyahu once put it, "America is a thing you can move very easily, move it in the right direction."[12]

American advocacy for Israel is also furthered through the politicization of Christians, especially those in evangelical circles. In the 1980s it was the so-called Moral Majority and more recently it is the Christian Coalition of America alongside Christians United for Israel that have vigorously lobbied for rather unqualified support of Israel. These Christian organizations have their own egoistic and ulterior motives for supporting Israel, namely their belief that the second coming of Christ will occur when Jews populate the Holy Land. This, they believe, will lead to Christian salvation, while the majority of Jews will be condemned to hell. While Israeli leaders view this theology with disdain, they welcome its political impact – a protective shield to guard Israel from reprimand and thereby enable its expansionist policies.

While aiding Israeli expansionism, the U.S. has continuously obstructed Palestinian efforts to work through international institutions and on the planes of international law. In 2012, for example, when an overwhelming majority of the UN voted in favor of Palestine attaining an "observer state" status in the international body, the U.S. voted against it. In 2014, it vetoed a UN Security Council motion to set a deadline for ending Israel's occupation. More recently, in 2021, the U.S. opposed an International Criminal Court investigation into the Palestinian situation. There are many more examples, but the ones listed here illustrate the point.

At this juncture it is fitting to present some considerations that are rarely, if ever, encountered in mainstream political discussions. It is often said that Israel is the U.S.'s most important ally in the fight against so-called Islamic terrorism. Arguably, however, it is exactly the other way around. Around the region, Israel is seen as an oppressor. Arguably, the U.S. has made itself a target for extremists, precisely because of its complicity in Israel's domination of the Palestinian people. At the same time, the people of the region abhor the U.S. support of brutal Arab authoritarian leaders, such as Abdel Fatah El-Sisi of Egypt or Mohammed bin Salman of Saudi Arabia. Terrorist groups like Al-Qaeda have cited such grievances as a motivation for their purported causes, including their acts against the U.S. and other Western countries. This, of course, is not to condone terrorism in any way, but it is important to give these considerations their place.

Israel also demands the U.S. join in its adversity against various Middle Eastern countries, such as Iraq or Iran. Often, this is serving Israeli interests but not U.S. interests. Regarding Iran, for example, there has been a long-standing concern about its nuclear ambitions. To abate these, in 2013, the Obama Administration began negotiations with Iran, which concluded in 2015 with the Joint Comprehensive Plan of Action (JCPOA). It entailed rigorous controls on Iran's feared nuclear program in exchange for the removal of international sanctions, thereby allowing the potential for Iran's reintegration into the global economy. The agreement was mutually beneficial. All along, however, Israel attempted to obstruct it and stand in the way of even slightly better relations between the U.S. and Iran. Once Trump assumed the presidency, the deal was canceled.

The central contention in this book has been that the strong do what they have the power to do. Israel, as the manifestly stronger side in the Israeli-Palestinian conflict, has indeed done as it willed. Throughout the book we have seen that external powers had a role in furnishing Israel with this power, and since the 1960s, it was the U.S. that has ensured Israel's power superiority across the region. A 2022 report by the Congressional Research Service summarizes:

> Israel is the largest cumulative recipient of U.S. foreign assistance since World War II … To date, the United States has provided Israel \$150 billion (current, or noninflation-adjusted, dollars) in bilateral

> assistance and missile defense funding. At present, almost all U.S. bilateral aid to Israel is in the form of military assistance; from 1971 to 2007, Israel also received significant economic assistance. In 2016, the U.S. and Israeli governments signed their third 10-year Memorandum of Understanding (MOU) on military aid, covering FY2019 to FY2028. Under the terms of the MOU, the United States pledged to provide—subject to congressional appropriation—$38 billion in military aid ($33 billion in Foreign Military Financing grants plus $5 billion in missile defense appropriations) to Israel.[13]

Regarding American money and arms, the former Israeli Defense Secretary Moshe Dayan once stated, "Our American friends offer us money, arms, and advice. We take the money, we take the arms and we decline the advice."[14] The American people, for their part, are often not aware of the large sums given to Israel. To the extent they are aware, they are given the impression that aiding Israel is furthering U.S. interests, and moreover that the interests of both countries are identical. The fact is that sometimes they are and sometimes they are not. This is normal in international relations. It is up to the reader to decide whether the U.S. should aid any country in the ways described here, especially when the receiving country itself is economically well off.

All this leads us to some ethical considerations about the U.S.'s strong support for Israel. Even to avid pro-Israel observers and advocates, it is evident that there is an increasing number of human rights reports that record the brutal conduct of Israeli security forces and settlers, endless suffering and misery of Palestinian people, and their subjection to arbitrary detentions, home demolitions, and dispossessions. Over the years, Israeli practices have culminated in it being declared an apartheid regime. In 2022, the former senior advisor to the Israeli government Daniel Levy warned at the UN Security Council that "the increasingly weighty body of scholarly, legal and public opinion that has designated Israel to be perpetuating apartheid ... must be a wake-up call." Israel could not have developed into an apartheid regime without U.S. acquiescence.

Overall, Americans continue to favor Israel. However, the work of social movements and the alliances between progressives, people of color, and Palestinian activists, as well as some elected representatives, has contributed to a shift in public awareness and discussions. Democrats and left-leaning independents as well as younger voters have come to develop more positive views of Palestinians over the last years. Noteworthy here is also the outlook of American Jews. Over the years, the Israeli government, as well as the polity, has moved ever further right. As discussed in Chapter 7, in late 2022 it elected the most far-right government in its history, with overtly racist orientations. It is thus not surprising that a growing number of Americans Jews are showing increasing concern over the direction of the country.

Notwithstanding these developments, the Biden Administration has continued with its strong support for Israel. Moreover, even as the world's leading human right organizations describe Israel as an apartheid regime and even as a legal case of genocide has been launched against Israel at the World Court as the year 2023 came to an end, the U.S continued with its provision of arms and munitions. Not surprisingly, the U.S. has drawn much international criticism for its positioning, much more so than usual. These go so far as the argument that it is complicit in a genocide.

Observers have put forth several suggestions for Washington leaders for a new course. Let us highlight just a few. Most importantly, Washington must come to reckon with the fact that it helped create a tragic reality, including the reality of Israeli apartheid. Instead of continuously emphasizing "unbreakable bonds" between the U.S. and Israel, Washington should advocate for human rights, equality, and citizenship for all inhabitants between the River and the Sea. Toward these ends, it should, for example, condition the nearly four billion dollars of aid that is given to Israel every year. At the same time, Washington should cease shielding Israel at international bodies like the UN or international courts. There are yet further suggestions, but what they all share is an insistence on holding Israel accountable.

Conclusion

Throughout this book I have stated Thucydides' famous and fundamental observation, namely that the strong do what they have the power to do. I should add here that, at times, they do it at their own peril. The preeminence of power and the neglect of justice have rendered Israel an apartheid state, with all the atrocities and ugliness this brings. Israelis may, for the moment, revel in their achievements of expanding the land of Israel ever more, but it is likely that history won't look favorably upon what happened. Palestinians, for their part, remain in utter desperation. This desperation has compelled their armed resistance, including acts of resistance in violation of international law. They will not cease to resist, as the Jewish Zionist Ze'ev Jabotinsky had forecasted 100 years ago. This is not a future either side can be looking forward to.

As we have seen throughout this book, this grim outlook was brought forth with the many-decades-long help of the U.S. and the acquiescence of the international community. As the world's superpower, the U.S. bears particular responsibility for shielding Israel from any accountability. Its policy of the last decades is in no one's interest. Neither is it morally defensible.

Suggested Further Readings

Barnett, Michael, Nathan Brown, Marc Lynch, and Shibley Tehami. 2023. *The One State Reality: What Is Israel/Palestine?* Ithaca, NY: Cornell University Press.

Boehm, Omri. 2021. *Haifa Republic: A Democratic Future for Israel.* New York: New York Review Books.

Ehrenberg, John and Yoav Peled. 2016. *Israel and Palestine: Alternative Perspectives on Statehood.* Lanham, MD: Rowman and Littlefield.

Gordis, Daniel. 2023. *Impossible Takes Longer: 75 Years After Its Creation, Has Israel Fulfilled Its Founders' Dreams?* New York: Ecco.

Halper, Jeff. 2021. *Decolonizing Israel, Liberating Palestine: Zionism, Settler Colonialism, and the Case for One Democratic State.* London: Pluto Press.

Lustick, Ian. 2019. *Paradigm Lost: From Two-State Solution to One-State Reality.* Philadelphia, PA: University of Pennsylvania Press.

Morris, Benny. 2009. *One State, Two States: Resolving the Israel/Palestine Conflict.* New Haven, CT: Yale University Press.

Sharif, Gershon. 2017. *A Half Century of Occupation.* Oakland, CA: University of California Press.

Tilley, Virginia. 2005. *The One-State Solution: A Breakthrough for Peace in the Israeli-Palestinian Deadlock.* Manchester: Manchester University Press.

Notes

1 Thucydides. 1972. *History of the Peloponnesian War.* New York: Penguin Books, p. 406.

2 Noura Erakat. 2019. *Justice for Some.* Stanford, CA: Stanford University Press, p. 9.

3 The White House. 2013. *Remarks of President Barack Obama to the People of Israel* (March 21). Available at https://obamawhitehouse.archives.gov/the-press-office/2013/03/21/remarks-president-barack-obama-people-israel

4 Quoted in the *Jerusalem Post* from January 26, 2010. Available at www.jpost.com/israel/pa-borders-are-our-greatest-threat

5 Quoted in *Haaretz* from November 29, 2007. Available at www.haaretz.com/2007-11-29/ty-article/olmert-to-haaretz-two-state-solution-or-israel-is-done-for/0000017f-e62a-dc7e-adff-f6af3bbe0000

6 Uri Avnery. 2008. *Israel's Vicious Cycle*, edited by Sara Powell. London: Pluto Press, p. 82.

7 Ilan Baruch and Alon Liel. 2021. *It's Apartheid, Say Israeli Ambassadors to South Africa* (June 8). Available at www.groundup.org.za/article/israeli-ambassadors-compare-israel-south-africa/

8 Associated Press. 2023. *A Former Mossad Chief Says Israel Is Enforcing an Apartheid System in the West Bank* (September 6). Available at https://apnews.com/article/israel-apartheid-palestinians-occupation-c8137c9e7f33c2cba7b0b5ac7fa8d115
9 Quoted in Benny Morris. 2009. *One State, Two States: Resolving the Israel/Palestine Conflict*. New Haven, CT: Yale University Press, p. 67.
10 Ilan Pappe. 2006. *The Ethnic Cleansing of Palestine*. Oxford: Oneworld Publications.
11 Peter Beinart. 2012. *The Crisis of Zionism*. New York: Picador, p. 24.
12 Quoted in Ian Lustick. 2019. *Paradigm Lost: From Two-State Solution to One-State Reality*. Philadelphia: PA: University of Pennsylvania Press, p. 61.
13 Congressional Research Service. 2022. *U.S. Foreign Aid to Israel* (February 18). Available at https://sgp.fas.org/crs/mideast/RL33222.pdf
14 Quoted in Avi Shlaim. 2014. *The Iron Wall*. New York: W.W. Norton, p. 320.

Index

Printed in the United States
by Baker & Taylor Publisher Services